ANDREW KUYVENHOVEN

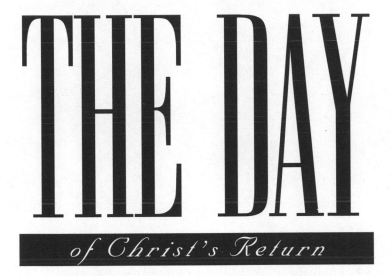

THE DAY
of Christ's Return

WHAT THE BIBLE TEACHES
WHAT YOU NEED TO KNOW

CRC Publications
Grand Rapids, Michigan

The Day of Christ's Return: What the Bible Teaches, What You Need to Know, © 1999 by CRC Publications, 2850 Kalamazoo Ave. SE, Grand Rapids, MI 49560.

All art ©SuperStock. Cover art: *Lion in Majesty* by Michele Giambono

Printed in the United States of America on recycled paper. ♻ 1-800-333-8300

Library of Congress Cataloging-in-Publication Data
Kuyvenhoven, Andrew.
     The day of Christ's return: what the bible teaches, what you need to know /
    Andrew Kuyvenhoven.
        p.   cm.
    Includes bibliographical references.
    ISBN 1-56212-374-2
     1. Second Advent—Biblical teaching. I. Title.
    BT886.K88 1999
    236'.9—dc21   98-41235
                                            CIP

10 9 8 7 6 5 4 3 2

CONTENTS

INTRODUCTION

"The night is nearly over; the day is almost here."
Romans 13:12

A Tough Topic

The day we discuss in this book is the one on which Jesus will come back to earth. All our days will climax on the Day. We don't live for today but for the Day. We're supposed to keep thinking about the day when the Son of Man will come "in a cloud with power and great glory" (Luke 21:27). In fact, we have been warned that we should not party too much nor worry too much because when we are "weighed down with dissipation, drunkenness and the anxieties of life . . . that day will close on you unexpectedly" (Luke 21:34). "The day of the Lord will come like a thief in the night" (1 Thess. 5:2), that is, without warning. When you live in expectation of the Lord, "this day" will not "surprise you like a thief," but you will be happy when "the day dawns" (2 Pet. 1:19).

This day is the subject of this book. It's a fascinating topic. Yet no matter how hard I try, I find it impossible to imagine the arrival of Jesus and all the events that are associated with his coming. When I try to imagine "the glorious appearing of our great God and Savior, Jesus Christ" (Titus 2:13), the best I can do is a sort of Star Trek kind of event, a space fantasy. I see a tremendous light, like a falling star, approaching the earth at great speed. It must be visible all over the globe. All of Mexico City, all of Canada, and a billion people in India see the light. When the blazing torch comes closer, we see a Person. And with a shattering noise the whole world is suddenly confronted with the Ultimate Reality. But when I am that far into my fantasy, I say to myself, you take the film industry too seriously.

It's not only the event of the Lord's coming that's impossible to imagine. The other happenings that are associated with his coming are totally baffling. "For the trumpet will sound, the dead will be raised imperishable, and we will be changed" (1 Cor. 15:52). The "we" who are to be changed are believers who are alive on that day. They will turn from mortal, fragile children of dust into gloriously immortal, recreated beings. It will happen "in a flash, in the twinkling of an eye" (v. 52), faster than you can say "converted into another mode of existence." And then they'll meet all those who fell asleep in the Lord, millions more.

But to say that our forebears are "sleeping" and waiting for the alarm clock to go off is nonsense, of course. Sorry, it's not nonsense, but it is an allegorical way of speaking that we may not take literally. You and I know very well that the bodies of our grandparents and their parents have returned to earth and dust—completely. As a matter of fact, the bodies of people who died long ago have been transformed into other bodies. They are in the cycle of organisms where dying and becoming food for other life is a well-known, age-old phenomenon. The bodies of the saints are irretrievably in the cycle. But the Bible says that on the day they will stand on their feet because the Voice will command them to do so. I find it unimaginable.

All who ever lived on this planet will rise when the Voice calls them. "Those who have done good will rise to live, and those who have done evil will rise to be condemned" (John 5:29). Parts of our small planet are overpopulated right now. On that day billions who died will be added to the living. All of us will stand before the Lord, the Bible says. There won't be standing room for all, one would think. And then what happens? Must all of us appear before the Judge? How many centuries will pass before your or my turn comes to stand before the Judge's chair?

End-Time Language

It's not only impossible to imagine the coming of Christ and the events associated with his coming, but the language in which the Bible tells us about these happenings is also painfully difficult. Bible students call it "eschatological" and "apocalyptic" language. That means it is language used to describe the end, the *eschaton*. Apocalyptic language is employed when the unutterable is put into pictures and written down in a book. It's about stars falling like rotten apples and animals of grotesque shapes scaring the daylights out of us. It's the extreme terror described in howling nights of horror.

The last book of the Bible is called the Apocalypse. Many wise Bible scholars, such as John Calvin and Martin Luther, have never written a commentary on that book. But many unwise people explain it as if they have next week's answer to this week's crossword puzzle.

No matter how our imagination fails and no matter how difficult it is to make sense of the images in the Book, we must think of the day. Christ's final coming to bring us full salvation is a major promise and a central teaching of the New Testament. One might say that Jesus hung the validity of his claims on two predictions: the destruction of Jerusalem and his return as "the Son of Man," who has received the everlasting kingdom from God himself. Jerusalem has been destroyed in A.D. 70, and the temple religion has been replaced with the worship of God through the blood and the Spirit of Christ. But we are still expecting "the day of the Son of Man."

Coming Soon

Every fresh reading of the New Testament leaves us not only with the message that Christ is coming but with the urgent news that he is coming *soon*. When Paul writes his letter to the Christians living in the capital of the Roman Empire, he writes this amazing sentence: "Our salvation is nearer now than when we first believed. The night is nearly over; the day is almost here" (Rom. 13:11-12). The astonishing thing is that he wrote these words in the year A.D. 57. He thought that in the year 57 they were closer to the return of the Lord than "when they first believed"—say, less than twenty years before that date. It's like a person in the city of Toronto, Ontario, taking two steps in a southern direction in his living room and then saying, I am now a lot closer to Miami, Florida, than before I took these steps.

In church magazines and table talks we like to discuss the church's "problems." We write and speak of worldliness creeping in and of too little gospel truth shining out. We wonder what will happen to the Christian church in Europe and we ask each other if the North American era is coming to a close. Is God moving his candlesticks to Asia and Africa? We continue our debates about the role of women in the church and the influence of the charismatic movement on every denomination. But writers and talkers, myself included, usually fail to realize that the biggest problem of the church of Jesus Christ is that her Lord has not yet returned!

The not-yet-fulfillment of Jesus' promise to return is also the biggest test of our faith. Do we really believe that he will come? And can we persist in prayer until he comes?

Good and Evil (detail of evil)

—Victor Orsel, 1795-1850

CHAPTER 1

THE BEGINNING OF THE END

Every book of the New Testament refers to the second coming of Christ, except for the two short notes we call 2 John and 3 John.

Since the coming of Jesus is at the heart of the Christian faith, the expectation of the Lord must live in the heart of everyone who keeps the faith. By definition, a Christian is forward-looking. We live by hope. The New Testament closes with a promise—"I am coming soon"—and a prayer—"Come, Lord Jesus" (Rev. 22:20). That promise is always on the mind of the church and that prayer lives in her heart.

The Old Testament is also forward-looking. The first promise followed the first sin (Gen. 3:15). Humanity would not always be deceived by the evil one; in the battle with the brood of the serpent, the offspring of the woman would win. When God called one man to become the father of all people, God promised that through Abraham's seed all the families of the earth would be blessed (Gen. 12:3). Since the days of Abraham, God's people travel as pilgrims. Their horizons are aglow with the promises of God.

God made a covenant with the liberated slaves Moses led out of Egypt (Ex. 19-20). They broke the covenant and were punished for it. But God promised a new covenant (Jer. 31:31). Israel wanted a king and got a king, but the king disobeyed God and brought disaster on Israel. Yet God promised a future King, a good Ruler, an everlasting King (2 Sam. 7:14; Isa. 9:6-7; Ps. 110:1).

In great anger, God allowed Assyria and Babylonia to murder his people and to destroy his temple. Yet God promised a restoration of life and land and a better future for Israel.

The Old Testament closes with a vision of the day of the Lord (Mal. 4). "Surely the day is coming; . . . the sun of righteousness will rise with healing in its wings . . ." (vv. 1-3). Then the wicked will be trampled but you will be so happy that "you will go out and leap like calves released from the stall" (v. 2).

The Old Testament believers lived by hope in the great future of God. In the New Testament that future became the present. But the end of one era was also a new beginning.

The Incomplete Fulfillment

The dawn of the sun of righteousness (Mal. 4:2) occurred with the birth of Jesus. In him the hope of the Old Testament became reality. But the New Testament revealed something for which the Old had not prepared God's people: there would be two comings of the Lord, one an appearance of grace and the other an appearance of glory. Christ came first in the form of a servant who "humbled himself and became obedient to death—even death on a cross!" (Phil. 2:8). He died, but he arose from death. Then "God exalted him to the highest place and gave him the name that is above every name, that at the name of Jesus every knee should bow . . . and every tongue confess that Jesus Christ is Lord, to the glory of God the Father" (Phil. 2:9-11). Today we kneel before Jesus. We confess him as Lord. But we must wait until he comes with glory before all knees will bow and all tongues confess. Only then will God's kingdom fill the world with everlasting peace.

The great future promised in the Old Testament has partially come because the Messiah came. However, it's only when he comes the second time that all the promises will be fulfilled.

The Old Testament does not distinguish between the first and the second comings of God in Christ. Old Testament believers saw the two comings as one event. Just as we cannot distinguish between two mountain peaks when we view them from a distance, so the Old Testament sees the two as one. We know that there's a long distance between the first and the second mountain. We travel between the two peaks, the two comings of the Lord. God's promises *have been* fulfilled and God's promises *will be* fulfilled. We have been redeemed *already.* But we are *not yet* in the new country. Christ won the victory *already* but the war is *not yet* over.

Jesus Christ has not yet returned. Yet he is not absent.

We are not living in a world without Jesus. We await his coming but we are not abandoned. And we must say of his kingdom what we confess of the King: His kingdom is here *and* it is coming.

Jesus Is Here and He Is Coming

Since, when Jesus left, he said, "I am with you" (Matt. 28:20), we should not say that the Lord is absent. He is present in a different way than when he walked and talked in Galilee. Today the Lord Jesus is present by the Holy Spirit. As such, he stays with us until the end of this age. Then we will see our glorified Savior and we too will be glorified. "When he appears, we shall be like him, for we shall see him as he is" (1 John 3:2).

"It is for your good that I am going away," said Jesus to his disciples. "Unless I go away, the Counselor will not come to you; but if I go, I will send him to you" (John 16:7).

The progression of salvation history brings advantages. Today we know Jesus better than the disciples did before the day of Pentecost, for it is the Spirit who opens our eyes for the beauty of our Lord, our ears for his Word, and our hearts for his entrance.

Through the Spirit Jesus is with us without interruption. The disciples knew moments of great panic because Jesus was absent. When they were alone in the boat, buffeted by waves, and when they saw the ghost as a sure sign of approaching death, they cried out in fear (Matt. 14:22-27). When the traitor, Judas, came with the crowd that arrested Jesus, "everyone deserted him and fled" (Mark 14:50). However, after Pentecost, when Jesus' presence became continuous through the Spirit, these same disciples were fearless in the crowd, sang hymns in prison, and died in hope. And we can do the same, because Jesus is with us continually.

Through the Spirit, Jesus is with us universally. During his earthly ministry, Jesus traveled less than a hundred miles. But since he ascended to God's throne and leads the great mission, he covers the globe by his Word and Spirit. He sends his willing servants. And when people receive those who have been sent, they really respond to the Sender, to Jesus (Matt. 10:40; John 20:21).

Certainly Jesus is present today. Every first day of the week since the resurrection of Jesus, we have been meeting as Christian congregations. And whenever we come together in his name, he is with us (Matt. 18:20).

To our shame, we confess that we, the members of Christ's church, have fought each other about the question of *how* our Savior is present in the Lord's Supper. But none of us wants to deny that we truly meet him in holy communion whenever we break bread and drink wine as he told us to do.

In this present dispensation, Jesus is here without glamour and sometimes without dignity. Unexpectedly we meet him in one who has no food, or shelter, or home, or country. But he himself will never forget what we do to the least of these relatives of his, because we do to Jesus what we do to them (Matt. 25:31-46).

Jesus is always present but he is never visible to our eyes. What *is* visible, however, are the bad things: crimes, wars, sickness, death, and all of the evil he came to remove. Even in the most blessed Christian life there's enough misery to make us long for a complete redemption and for Jesus to be tangibly present. We don't deny that he is here, but we pray that he be "unveiled," revealed as Lord and Savior. We "eagerly wait for our Lord Jesus Christ to be revealed" (1 Cor. 1:7). He has glory already. He is Lord. But we pray that this reality, which is unseen and widely denied in the present dispensation, will be manifested. Then we will be together with him as we are now (Rom. 8:38-39), but in a different mode, in glory.

God's Kingdom Is Here and It Is Coming

What we have just said of the person of Jesus, we may also say of his kingdom: it invaded this world at his first coming, and it will be fully consummated when he comes again. It is *here* and it is *coming*, just as he is here and he is coming.

The kingdom is the blessed rule of God that entered into the world through Jesus when he threw out the demons and forgave sinners. "The kingdom of God has come upon you" (Matt. 12:28), he said, because the Spirit of God, who was in Jesus, proved stronger than the devil, who occupied the land and who held people in bondage.

The demons knew Jesus. "Have you come here to torture us before the appointed time?" (Matt. 8:29). Actually their final hour had not yet come. Jesus allowed the demons to continue their destructive work for a season. He sent them into the herd of pigs. But the wild man who was possessed by a legion of demons was saved. He was dressed and he looked healthy (Mark 5:1-20; see also Matt. 8:28-34).

The final hour had not yet come, but Jesus did win the decisive battle. "I saw Satan fall like lightning from heaven," said Jesus, when seventy-two of his followers performed their first assignment on behalf of the kingdom of God (Luke 10:18).

Already, but Not Yet

God used Paul to explain that the decisive battle in the ongoing war took place in the death and resurrection of Jesus. The death of Jesus was the final judgment. Here the wrath of God was poured out. God punished sinful humanity in the One who represented the many (Rom. 8:1, 3; 2 Cor. 5:21). That was *the end.* "One died for all, and therefore all died" (2 Cor. 5:14).

And the resurrection was *the beginning* of the new age. The new world has actually come for all who are "in Christ." "The old has gone, the new has come!" (2 Cor. 5:17). Anyone who is in Christ is already part of a new creation, even if we continue to carry the new treasure in jars of clay (2 Cor. 4:7). And even if we are "being given over to death for Jesus' sake" (v. 11), we live by faith in Christ and "we fix our eyes not on what is seen, but on what is unseen" (v. 18).

This teaching of the New Testament is the big surprise for those who waited for the kingdom according to the prophecies of the Old Testament. The Old Testament did not teach that the coming of the kingdom would first require a series of events: the death and resurrection of the Messiah, then two millennia of gospel preaching and divine compassion, and God only knows what more, before Christ's glory is revealed.

Both the Messiah and the kingdom are divinely different from what anyone expected. And yet, once we know Jesus as the Christ and ourselves as his own, we can see that all things happened "according to the Scriptures" (1 Cor. 15:3), and that the gospel of the kingdom is the beginning of the end.

Jewish Expectation and Response

Most Jews find it impossible to believe that the Messiah has already come. Some years ago, a great Jewish philosopher, Martin Buber, expressed the reason for Jewish unbelief in a memorable way during a discussion with Karl L. Schmidt. "You cannot convince us that the Messiah has come," said Buber,

---

Our small children already know that Jesus came into the world to suffer and die for our sins. They know the mystery of the Messiah. And they may grow old without ever realizing that a suffering and dying King of Israel on a cross is an impossible folly to many.

One of the novels of Chaim Potok is *My Name Is Asher Lev*. Asher Lev grows up in a Brooklyn community of Hasidic Jews. He has the gift of drawing and painting, which brings him fame and rejection. One day Asher and his mother make the forbidden trip to the museum. There Asher meets artistic representations of Christ's suffering.

"Can you explain those paintings to me, Mama?"

"The first ones we saw?"

"Yes."

"They were about a man called Jesus." . . .

"I know about Jesus," I said. "Jesus is the God of the goyim" [Gentiles].

"Jesus was a Jew who lived in Eretz Yisroel [the land of Israel] at the time of the Romans. The Romans killed him. That was the way Romans executed people. They hung them from those big poles, the way you saw in the paintings."

"Were many Jews killed by the Romans?"

"Thousands. Tens of thousands."

"Why did the Romans kill Jesus?

"He said he was the Moshiach [Messiah]. They thought he would make a revolution against them."

"Was he the Moshiach, Mama?"

"No. He was not the Moshiach. The Moshiach has not yet come, Asher. Look how much suffering there is in the world. Would there be so much suffering if the Moshiach had really come?"

—Chaim Potok, *My Name Is Asher Lev*, pp. 162-163

"because everyone can see that this world is still unredeemed" (Jürgen Moltmann, *The Way of Jesus Christ,* p. 28, and G. C. Berkouwer, *The Return of Christ,* p. 129).

The way in which Martin Buber expected the coming of the Messiah—in one great, liberating event—does not differ from the way John the Baptizer expected it. That's because Mr. Buber and John the Baptizer both still belong to the Old Testament.

John the Baptizer—or "the Baptist" as English translations keep calling him—has his job description in Isaiah 40:3: "In the desert prepare the way of the LORD" (see Matt. 3:3; Mark 1:3; Luke 3:4). But when John himself refers to the One for whom he is working, he speaks somewhat mysteriously about "the one who comes after me" (John 1:27). Without a doubt, his Jewish audience understood John to be speaking of the Messiah. John described the Messiah as the Mighty One and the Worthy One, whose sandals he was hardly permitted to carry.

John prepared the way for his Lord by preaching a baptism of repentance for the forgiveness of sins (Mark 1:4). The work of the Coming One he described as the baptism "with the Holy Spirit and with fire" (Matt. 3:11). In John's mouth these words do not refer to a marvelous experience but to the fiery furnace of God's final judgment. That's why the next verse reads, "His winnowing fork is in his hand, and he will clear his threshing floor, gathering his wheat into the barn and burning up the chaff with unquenchable fire" (Matt. 3:12). John the Baptizer announced the coming of the kingdom of heaven as the final judgment in which evil and evildoers would be done away with, but when those who repented and believed would be saved.

The Unbelief of Buber and the Frustration of the Baptizer

John the Baptizer ended up in prison, but not because he was a criminal. Wherever tyrants rule, good people pine in prison. John told Herod that he had no right to cohabit with his brother's wife. That sermon put John in prison and finally cost him his head.

John was a great and fearless prophet—the greatest in fact—according to the word of Jesus (Matt. 11:11). But while he was incarcerated, John wasn't worried about his own life, but whether Jesus was really the Messiah. He worried because he did not see the fire and the ax of the Lord which he, John himself, had announced and expected.

"Are you the one who was to come, or should we expect someone else?" (Matt. 11:3). That was John's question to Jesus.

Jesus' answer deserves careful study, especially by Gentiles who have become Christians. We believe the New Testament and we think we know it. But we often forget that we must also know the Bible of John the Baptizer and Martin Buber. For when we are Christians we belong to a Jewish family that reads a Jewish book and we are saved by a Jewish Messiah. Even the New Testament is full of allusions to the Old. Unless we know the Old, we miss all the finer points of the New.

We catch the meaning of Jesus' answer if we first read Isaiah 35, the poem about the land of hope and glory that will become reality when "your God will come" (v. 4). The desert will blossom, the hearts of the fearful will be vibrant with hope. The blind will see and the deaf will hear, the lame will leap and the mute will sing. The dry place will be a river and ruins will turn to pastures. Sorrow and sighing will flee away. Isaiah 35 pictures the country of Israel's dreams. This is God's kingdom. It is paradise restored.

Jesus answered John's disciples, "Go back and report to John what you hear and see: the blind receive sight, the lame walk, those who have leprosy are cured, the deaf hear, the dead are raised, and the good news is preached to the poor. Blessed is the man who does not fall away on account of me" (Matt. 11:4-6).

Jesus was saying that the great future had come! The blind see, the lame leap, and death departs at his command. But his last phrase, which comes from Isaiah 61:1, is the climax: "Good news is preached to the poor." The *poor* are the oppressed people of God. They hope for God's kingdom and they have nothing else to hope for. Now they receive the good news, "the gospel of the kingdom" (Matt. 24:14).

Jesus adds a warning: "Blessed is the man who does not fall away on account of me" (Matt. 11:6). That means, in this connection, blessed is the person, and blessed is John, if he does not reject me because of the way in which I bring the kingdom of heaven to earth.

We have no record of John's reaction to Jesus' message. But Martin Buber and his friends seem to say: You aren't the Coming One. If you were the Messiah, the world would have been redeemed at your coming. We wait for someone else, they say.

The Secret of the Messiah

Jesus is the Messiah (Christ, in Greek), which means "Anointed One." He is the promised King of Israel on whom the Spirit rests. "Jesus is the Messiah" is the oldest confession of those who were later called Christians.

In the beginning of his ministry on earth, Jesus revealed himself to his disciples by his teaching and by his works. Then he asked the big question, "Who do people say I am?" (Mark 8:27). In all three gospels this question is the conclusion and high point of the first part of Jesus' ministry (Matt. 16:13; Mark

8:27; Luke 9:18). The question is not only at the center of these writings, but by the answer to this question everyone will be judged.

Peter gave the right answer. According to Matthew, Peter replied, "You are the Christ, the Son of the living God" (16:16). Mark has, "You are the Christ" (8:29). Luke's version: "The Christ of God" (9:20).

The important word in the answer is *Christ* (in Hebrew, *Messiah).* Peter gave the right answer but he could not take credit for doing so. Flesh and blood had not revealed it. He did not find the answer by putting two and two together. No one knows the mystery of the Messiah but those to whom God reveals it.

"From that time on Jesus began to explain to his disciples that he must go to Jerusalem and suffer many things . . . and that he must be killed and on the third day be raised to life" (Matt. 16:21). So also in Mark 8:31, "He then began to teach them that the Son of Man must suffer many things . . ." (compare with Luke 9:21f.).

The teaching that the Messiah would have to suffer and die was unheard of. Peter, the man who had just recognized the Messiah in Jesus, vehemently objected to the announcement of suffering. But Jesus commanded: "Get behind me, Satan!" (Matt. 16:23). Jesus knows himself bound by a mandate from his Father and he knows that it is Satan who wants to keep him from this road of obedience. He tells Satan to get out of his way. All who do not agree with God's plan for bringing the kingdom by the way of servanthood, suffering, and the cross are the devil's advocates.

Throughout Jesus' earthly ministry, he faced one great temptation: to take a shortcut to glory. He was tempted to avoid obedience until death on the cross. That was the issue in the three temptations in the wilderness at the beginning of his ministry (Matt. 4:1-11; Luke 4:1-13). That was also the temptation in his agonizing struggle in the garden of Gethsemane. And that was the last temptation when the mockers around his cross cried: "Let this Christ, this King of Israel, come down now from the cross, that we may see and believe" (Mark 15:32). But he remained obedient. His loyalty to the Father and his love for us were the two nails that kept him on the cross until this phase of his work was "finished" (John 19:30). Against all expectations, but according to the will of God, Jesus was and is the crucified Messiah, who by love and suffering redeems and conquers the world.

The Heart of the Gospel of the Kingdom

Liberal teachers used to say that Jesus *thought* he was the Messiah of Israel. But when Israel rejected him, he accepted the way of the cross as God's will. Thereby he taught us valuable, moral lessons, they said. But they denied that he came into the world to offer himself as a sacrifice for our sins.

Today many evangelical teachers say that Jesus offered himself to Israel as the Messiah, but that Israel rejected him. Therefore the plans were modified. He became the suffering Messiah, who died to save all those who would believe in him—the church. But he will come back as the kind of Messiah Israel wanted in the first place, an earthly king in an earthly Jerusalem. At his second coming, they say, the nation will be converted to God. Israel will be independent and victorious over its enemies, while Messiah Jesus sits on David's throne for a thousand years. They consider the sacrifice of Jesus an intermezzo, an act that became necessary because of the unbelief of Israel.

I will address this teaching of dispensationalism in chapter 4. At this point it is important for us to realize that Christ's suffering is the only way for him to bring the kingdom. The cross is not a detour, as dispensationalists argue, after which Judaism gets its earthly king. But by his suffering and self-sacrifice Christ brings to us the kingdom and the glory. This is the kind of Messiah God has given us. And there is no other.

The Cross Is the Pacification of the Universe

Judaism does not have the cross, the symbol of suffering. But for the Christian religion the cross is central. On the cross Jesus offered the atoning sacrifice for the sins of the world (1 John 2:2). The cross of Jesus Christ is the means by which the whole universe is reconciled to God.

Christ is the Savior of the individual believer, the Jew first, but also the Gentile. Everyone may and must confess personally, "[He] loved me and gave himself for me" (Gal. 2:20). However, the individual is always part of "the

---

In Potok's novel *My Name Is Asher Lev,* when Asher matures as a man and a painter, he becomes famous with a painting that his agent calls "Brooklyn Crucifixion." In it he uses the symbol of the cross and his mother as the crucified one—to express her agony due to her husband and her son:

> I painted swiftly in a strange nerveless frenzy of energy. For all the pain you suffered, my mama. For all the torment of your past and future years, my mama. For all the anguish this picture of pain will cause you. . . . For the Master of the Universe, whose suffering world I do not comprehend . . . for all these I created this painting—an observant Jew working on a crucifixion because there was no aesthetic mold in his own religious tradition into which he could pour a painting of ultimate anguish and torment.

—Chaim Potok, *My Name Is Asher Lev,* p. 313

body," and apart from the body of Christ, no one can have the benefits of Christ. "For we were all baptized by one Spirit into one body—whether Jews or Greeks, slave or free—and we were all given the one Spirit to drink" (1 Cor. 12:13), the Spirit of Christ.

But having said that, we have not yet exhausted the scope of Christ's saving work. "Through him [God was pleased] to reconcile to himself all things, whether things on earth or things in heaven, by making peace through his blood, shed on the cross" (Col. 1:20). That means that Christ went to the cross to pacify the whole rebellious cosmos. It pleased God to restore creation through the sacrifice of Jesus, so that the universe should be what he intended it to be from the beginning. And Christ himself is the heart and harmony of the cosmos. "In him all things hold together" (v. 17).

This situation, the restored dominion of God over creation, reconciled by the cross, is the kingdom for which we pray and work.

The mystery of this kingdom is not, as the dispensationalists say, that the kingdom of David's Son was postponed on behalf of the church age. But the mystery of the kingdom is the mystery of the King. He had to suffer and die. Only by being lifted up on a cross (John 12:32) would he draw all people to himself. The cross is the heart of the Christian religion. No one who wants to bypass the cross can enter into the kingdom.

According to Jesus, John the Baptizer, who expected the kingdom of God as the judgment on evil and the removal of wickedness, was still the greatest of all Old Testament prophets. He was the greatest of all, "yet he who is least in the kingdom of heaven is greater than he" (Matt. 11:11). In this sentence greatness must not be understood in a moral sense, like being courageous. Greatness must be understood in the light of the history of salvation. As it is used here, greatness depends on one's closeness to Jesus.

In the long row of Old Testament prophets, John was the last and *therefore* the greatest. The others saw from afar. But John could stretch out his hand and say, There he is, the Messiah! Compared with the Old Testament prophets, none was greater than John because none was closer to Jesus.

But the least in the kingdom is greater than John, because any and every New Testament believer knows the Messiah more intimately than John could have known him. John knew that the Messiah would bring the judgment; we know how Christ had to bear that judgment. John knew that the wrath of God would be displayed; we know that the wrath of God was poured out on the Messiah! The least in the kingdom is greater than John because every New Testament believer knows a Messiah who died on the cross for us. We know the mystery that was hidden. It has now been revealed.

Four Horsemen of the Apocalypse

—Hans Holbein

CHAPTER 2

THE SURE PROMISE AND THE LONG WAIT

When a group of elders and preachers, myself included, examined a candidate for the ministry, I asked the would-be preacher, "Do you expect Christ to come at any time?"

"Yes, I do," said the candidate.

Another preacher asked, "But doesn't the Bible teach you that first the Antichrist must come and that we shall be persecuted for our faith before Jesus returns?"

"I guess so . . . , " said the candidate.

"Well, then," the same preacher insisted, "we should not teach that the return of Jesus is imminent, should we?"

"No," said the candidate, who was now confused and somewhat embarrassed, "we should not say that the Lord Jesus might come at any time."

The problem that the preachers were loading onto the candidate wasn't a real one. The gospel requires us to be ready to meet our Lord any year, any month, any week, any day, and any night. But as soon as we use predicted events to reduce our watchfulness and postpone our readiness for the time of his coming, we do something the Bible refuses to do. We draw conclusions based on our own calculations.

Jesus Taught Readiness

Some Christians, believing that the Lord Jesus knows everything, argue that he also knew that we would have to wait a very long time for his return. I do not doubt that Christ knew that there would be a time, an interim, between his resurrection and his return. That's why he founded his church (see ch. 3). And yet, he did *not* teach that we would have to wait for many centuries before he would come back.

Keep Watch

In the parables about a master who travels and a bridegroom who arrives later than expected, there may be some indication that Jesus was preparing his disciples for a long wait. The parable of the ten girls explains that "the bridegroom was a long time in coming" (Matt. 25:5). The unfaithful servant in Matthew 24:48 says, "My master is staying away a long time."

However, Jesus did not tell these stories in order to teach us that it would be a long time before he would return. The point of the parable about the stewards

Albert Schweitzer, the great theologian, musician, and medical doctor, has influenced Bible scholars with his theory that Jesus expected the kingdom of God to become a reality during his ministry. According to Schweitzer, when the great future did not come, Jesus died a martyr's death, crying, "My God, my God, why have you forsaken me?" (Matt. 27:46).

The argument for assuming that Jesus expected this present age to end soon and the kingdom of God to break through rests mainly on three sayings of Jesus:

- "When you are persecuted in one place, flee to another. I tell you the truth, you will not finish going through the cities of Israel before the Son of Man comes" (Matt. 10:23).

- "Some who are standing here will not taste death before they see the kingdom of God come with power" (Mark 9:1).

- "This generation will certainly not pass away until all these things have happened" (Mark 13:30).

These are difficult texts, although plausible interpretations have been suggested. The nearness of kingdom glory may refer to the glory of Christ that began with his resurrection. And in saying "this generation will not pass away," he may have meant "this kind of people," "people with this mentality." That's how Jesus used "this generation" on other occasions, as in Matthew 11:16; 12:41; and Mark 8:12. (See, for example, F. F. Bruce, *The Hard Sayings of Jesus.*)

It is certainly improper, as many have done, to use these three sayings as a basis for theories about a *delay* of the end of the age and about a "misconception" Jesus had. Christ said that the end would come as unexpectedly as a burglary, yet he gave signs of its coming and spoke of its *imminence.* These three features exist next to each other, and there is no evidence that the early church was bothered by them. Stephen H. Travis has rightly pointed out that the "imminence language of Jesus asserts that the age of decisive fulfilment has really dawned, the kingdom of God is being manifested here and now, and the present manifestations guarantee God's ultimate triumph through Christ" (*Christian Hope and the Future,* p. 90).

The same author has pointed out that Jesus uses visionary and poetic language in which an event may be pictured as imminent, while, strictly speaking, it is not (Travis, *I Believe in the Second Coming of Jesus,* p. 93).

is that they do not know when the master will return, and therefore they must be ready to receive him anytime.

The parable of the ten virgins does seem to deal with being prepared for a long wait. Five girls are "wise" precisely because they had counted on a longer waiting period. They brought enough oil for their lamps. But here too the conclusion is: "Therefore, keep watch, because you do not know the day or the hour" (Matt. 25:13).

The point is not so much the long wait as the uncertainty of the time of his coming.

Nowhere in the teaching of Jesus—in fact, nowhere in the New Testament—are we told that we might have to wait a very long time. The opposite is true. The coming of Jesus is near. He might come anytime. He will come soon.

Although it is never the explicit teaching of the New Testament that we will have to wait a long time for the return of the Lord, we are told repeatedly that we must be persistent and show endurance, which means that it might take longer than we expect. In his prophetic end-time speech Jesus also says that certain things must precede the end of the present age: "this gospel of the kingdom will be preached in the whole world as a testimony to all nations, and then the end will come" (Matt. 24:14). Similarly, Paul writes "that day will not come until the rebellion occurs and the man of lawlessness is revealed . . ." (2 Thess. 2:3). But as I will argue in later chapters, these few hints may not tempt us to write a calendar of future events. We are never allowed to think of the coming of Jesus as an event that might take place in a century or two. We may only think of his coming as *near.*

Coming Any Day

We have thirteen letters of Paul in the New Testament. By common consent, the letters to the church in Thessalonica are the oldest. They must have been written in the year A.D. 51, about twenty years after the death and resurrection of Jesus. These letters are largely devoted to eschatology, to teachings about the *last things* (the Greek word *eschaton* means "end").

The earliest readers of these letters, who were first-generation Christians, longed for the return of the Lord with an ardor that we just don't have any longer. They were sure that Jesus would come soon. They were literally expecting him anytime. But after living in this hope for a while, some of the members of the congregation died; they "fell asleep." And the Christians who buried their loved ones felt doubly sad. They experienced the common pain of death, but they also feared that the beloved departed, who had so often spoken of the day of the Lord, would miss the joy of the meeting. So Paul wrote to them that "[we] who are left to the coming of the Lord, will certainly not precede those who have fallen asleep" (1 Thess. 4:15).

Later we'll return to a discussion of this so-called rapture text. For now we want to realize that such a question can only arise in a community where people constantly ask themselves, "Will he come today? Shall we see him tomorrow?" Very few of us live in that kind of a Christian community.

Not that living in such an intense atmosphere of expectation is desirable in every respect. The Thessalonians were liable to believe rumors and they became "easily unsettled or alarmed by some prophecy or word or letter" to the effect "that the day of the Lord has already come" (2 Thess. 2:2). Because of their state of excitement they were susceptible to being "deceived" (2 Thess. 2:3). They were tempted to stop doing ordinary work and look at the sky. Paul told them not to be idle and reminded them of his rule, "If a man will not work, he shall not eat" (2 Thess. 3:10). Also in 1 Thessalonians 4:11-12 he reminds them to "work with [their own] hands" and so gain the respect of their neighbors.

It Can't Be Long Anymore

Paul never expected the present world to go on for twenty centuries when he said "salvation is nearer now than when we first believed. The night is nearly over; the day is almost here" (Rom. 13:11-12). He wrote this about twenty-five years after the resurrection of the Lord and about twenty years since the day when he "first believed." After twenty years he thought that he was significantly closer to the day of the Lord. But we read his words approximately one hundred times twenty years later and still the day is not here.

Paul shows a similar expectation of an early return of the Lord when he tells the Corinthians:

> The time is short. From now on those who have wives should live as if they had none; those who mourn, as if they did not; those who are happy, as if they were not; those who buy something, as if it were not theirs to keep; those who use the things of the world, as if not engrossed in them. For this world in its present form is passing away.
> —1 Corinthians 7:29-31

If we know that next month or next week this present mode of living will be history, we are going to be less concerned and less involved than when we think we must make a fortune in this life. Paul said that we should not cling to the present because it will soon be over, echoing what Jesus himself had said in Luke 21:34.

Paul really believed that the "time is short" (1 Cor. 7:29) and "the night is nearly over, the day is almost here" (Rom. 13:12). And when he wrote to the Philippians "the Lord is near" (4:5), he meant it in a temporal sense.

It seems undeniable that the apostle Paul expected an early return of Jesus. Another question is whether he changed his mind during his ministry. Some scholars believe that at first he was quite confident that the day of Christ would come during his lifetime. It was his own preaching, they say, that caused the anxiety in the congregation of Thessalonica. They did not know what to believe about people who died before the great day. And when Paul answered their questions, he said, "the dead in Christ will rise first" (1 Thess. 4:16). But he still figured that he would live until Christ's coming because he counts himself in when he says "we who are still alive, who are left till the coming of the Lord . . ." (1 Thess. 4:15). Also, in 1 Corinthians 15 Paul says, "the dead will be raised imperishable, and we [who are still alive] will be changed" (v. 52). Yet in later letters, these Bible students say, Paul does not speak of being changed when Christ comes. He speaks of going to heaven when he dies. When he writes the letter to the Philippians he is ready "to depart and be with Christ" (1:23). And in his last letter, 2 Timothy, he counts on dying before Christ's coming (4:6-8).

We should note that

- Paul did expect an early return of the Lord.

- he never made the time of Christ's coming a part of his gospel.

- Paul's use of *we* in "we will be changed" (1 Cor. 15:52) does not necessarily imply a personal conviction that he would be alive at the coming of the Lord. During the same year in which he wrote 1 Corinthians, he wrote 2 Corinthians 5:1-10. There he speaks of "the earthly tent we dwell in" and how "we long to be clothed with our heavenly dwelling." In other words, during the period in which he supposedly counted on living until the return of the Lord, as some people say, he could also contemplate being with the Lord in heaven, *before* the day would arrive (2 Cor. 5).

Always Coming Soon

The Lord is coming "soon," "quickly," and "without delay." That's the word of promise.

The serpent will soon be crushed, says Paul. Already in paradise, God promised that the serpent would be crushed by the Child of the woman (Gen. 3:15). It's impossible to say how many centuries elapsed between that word and Paul's writing in Romans 16:20: "The God of peace will soon crush Satan under your feet." That's a beautiful text. "God of peace" Paul calls God, because God is the Source of *shalom,* which comes to earth in Jesus. He will make all people and all creation whole and healthy. Then there will be peace. The great disturber of the peace, Satan, the old serpent, will be crushed by God under our feet. God will use our feet to stamp on him. So Christians are involved with head, mouth, hands, and feet in the establishment of peace on earth and war on evil. God works through us, and the work will "soon" be finished.

How should we understand *soon?* It refers to time, doesn't it? All who hunger for righteousness and cry for justice must wonder how to interpret the *soon* of God's promise.

The book of Revelation (called "The Apocalypse") was written to show Christ's servants "what must soon take place" (Rev. 1:1). The book closes with the promise: "Yes, I am coming soon," to which the church replies, "Amen, come Lord Jesus" (Rev. 22:20).

The church is tempted to explain away this "soon" of the promise by saying that it was a mistake. Many of us believe that the Lord is not "near" in the sense that his coming is soon to be expected, but that he is near in space, that he is not far removed. Many Bible teachers have made this switch explicitly or implicitly.

All of us who wait for the coming of Jesus look a bit quaint in the eyes of the ordinary citizens of this present world. We're as odd as Blumhardt. "Blumhardt," Frederick Buechner writes in the Foreword to this book of poetry, is "presumably some legendary Dutch eccentric." He keeps his horse and carriage in perpetual readiness so that when Christ comes again in his glory, he, Blumhardt, will be able to drive to meet him in a proper conveyance and properly attired in "his tall hat and Sunday best."

His coach stood ready all his whole life long
with horse, reins, and robe, in case the time
should be fulfilled in which the angels' song
would ring out gloriously, then he would climb
into his seat—tall hat and Sunday best—
sitting up straight, he would go trotting forth
to meet his Lord, who'd surely come at last—
and now for good—as King of all the earth.
O God, what have you done with such a heart,
so full of homesickness and such great dreams?
He now lies still and waiting in the ground.
What will you do with all of us who wait
in this dark age, longing for your return,
calling to you with pleading, doubtful sound?

—"Blumhardt" from *So Much Sky*, Jan Willem Schulte Nordholt;
trans. by Henrietta Ten Harmsel; © 1994, Wm. B. Eerdmans
Publishing Co. Used by permission.

A more radical reaction would be to write off all of the promises because this central one remains unfulfilled. God forbid that any one of us should do it! But it *is* fair to acknowledge that here lies the greatest problem of the church. The greatest problem for all believing Christians is the fact that the Lord Jesus has not yet come back, while we have been promised for two thousand years that he'll be coming soon. Yet the Bible never says that Christ's delay is the difficulty—it's our ability to remain alert that's in doubt.

Can We Hold Out Until He Comes?

The parable of the persistent widow in Luke 18:1-8 brings together the call for endurance—it might take a long time—and the promise that the Lord will come quickly.

Jesus teaches that we should always pray and not give up. He tells of a woman who had been done an injustice. Maybe someone had taken away her possessions, perhaps her house. The callous judge did not care to do anything because a weak widow carried no clout. But this woman kept coming to the judge, asking for justice: "Grant me justice against my adversary" (v. 3). I imagine she was the first one-person picket outside of the courthouse. Finally the judge replied, I better do something, because she will drive me mad.

The Lord asks us to notice that a persistent widow can wear out a callous judge. How much more should we be persistent in asking the other Judge who has always defended the rights of the weak and the widows? He listens when his loved ones "cry out to him day and night[.] Will he keep putting them off?" Jesus asks. "I tell you, he will see that they get justice, and quickly" (Luke 18:7-8).

Here Christ speaks of a delay, although the end of verse 7 is hard to translate and therefore we may not hang too much onto it. Certainly the point of Christ's teaching is *not* that God will delay but that we should persistently pray.

The strange combination in this parable is that we must learn to be persistent in prayer, asking again and again, *and* we must believe that the Lord answers quickly, speedily. Apparently the fact that he will answer quickly does not take away our obligation to pray persistently.

The story ends with a very serious, unanswered question: "However, when the Son of Man comes, will he find faith on the earth?" (Luke 18:8). Faith, in this connection, means the prayerful persistence of the widow who cries day and night, "Grant me justice against my adversary" (v. 3). The serious question is not whether God will answer or whether Jesus will come. The question is whether we will still be crying to the Judge of heaven and earth when he does. Or will we have given up and given in to the desires and the powers of this world? The Judge will do justice. He will vindicate God's children and deliver them from oppression. He will do it quickly. But can we persist until he comes?

Wait a Little Longer

Parallel to the story of the persistent widow is the vision of the souls of those who had been slain and the cry of the martyrs in Revelation 6:9-11.

> When [the Lamb] opened the fifth seal, I saw under the altar the souls of those who had been slain because of the word of God and the testimony they had maintained. They called out in a loud voice, "How long, Sovereign Lord, holy and true, until you judge the inhabitants of the earth and avenge our blood?" Then each of them was given a white robe, and they were told to wait a little longer, until the number of their fellow servants and brothers who were to be killed as they had been was completed.
>
> —Revelation 6:9-11

The blood of the martyrs—their "souls," which, like the blood of the slain sacrifice drips to the base of the altar—cries out to heaven for justice. And in response we have that same mixture of a call for endurance and a promise of quick action. They have to "wait a little longer" until the quota of martyrdom is filled up; only a "little longer."

The cry of those who have seen injustice and cruelty has gone up to heaven since Abel was slain by his selfish and evil brother Cain (Gen. 4:10). "How long?" God's people have said it almost since the beginning of time. "How long, O LORD? Will you forget me forever?" (Ps. 13:1). Four times this psalm asks, "How long?" "Vindicate me, O God, and plead my cause . . . " (Ps. 43:1).

Of course, God has responded to these cries by the great intervention of Jesus Christ himself. He came to rescue the poor, the pure in heart, and all who hunger and thirst for righteousness. "Blessed are the poor in spirit," he said, "for theirs is the kingdom of heaven" (Matt. 5:3). He took their side, and as the sacrificial Lamb of God he permitted his own blood to drip from the altar. But the blood of Jesus does not cry for revenge and retribution. His blood speaks of forgiveness and reconciliation (Heb. 12:24).

That gives us a hint why his coming to do justice seems delayed. It's not really that God is slow, but he is patient and merciful, "not wanting anyone to perish, but everyone to come to repentance" (2 Pet. 3:9).

A Single Hint

Only one Bible passage directly addresses our concern about the not-yet-fulfilled promise of Christ's return. It's 2 Peter 3:3-13. "Scoffers [say] where is this 'coming' he promised? Ever since our fathers died everything goes on as it has since the beginning of creation" (2 Pet. 3:4).

But these scoffers overlook the flood, says the writer. God's Word created a world out of water and the Word that destroyed the world by water is the same Word that today preserves the world for the fire of judgment (vv. 5-7).

Furthermore, the writer wants us to think of God's being and character (vv. 8-9). With the Lord, a day is like a thousand years and a thousand years are like a day. We miss the point when we think of God as being slow. Rather, he is patient and loving. He is holding back the fiery judgment because he wants all people to repent (v. 9).

Second Peter is a book that is younger than nearly all books of the New Testament, while its authorship is suspect for various reasons. This has led many Bible scholars to argue that the passage in 2 Peter came from the need to "explain" the return that did not happen. These scholars find that the passage confirms their own theory that originally, Christ and his followers expected a speedy coming of the everlasting kingdom. But when that did not happen, Christianity became a religious institution, a church organization busy with its own maintenance but no longer expecting a new age and an everlasting kingdom.

The passsage does present difficulties. When we are promised that the return of the Lord is "near" and that he is coming "soon," words are used that have meaning in our view of time. "Near" is not far. "Soon" is not late. I don't think 2 Peter is trying to change the meaning of these words. But we may not place this "near" in a calculation from which we conclude that the Lord is "slow in keeping his promise." If we do that, we end up in the seat of the scoffers.

Rather, we must keep in mind that it is God who made the promise, and God's view of time is not ours. Second, the time of the event cannot be calculated because "the day of the Lord will come like a thief" (v. 10). Finally, we must learn that the long wait does not mean that God is indifferent or "slow." No, the long wait shows God's love and patience aimed at humanity's conversion.

In a sense, therefore, it's not just *we* who are waiting. God is waiting also (see Berkouwer, *The Return of Christ,* p. 124). God is still restraining the judgment by which the present heavens and earth must be given up and replaced. Today is the interim. It's the time of our mission, the day of grace, the last opportunity for all people to wake up and let Christ shine on them.

God wants the world to be saved, and we must work and pray for the same thing. We must pray "for kings and all those in authority, that we may live peaceful and quiet lives in all godliness and holiness. This is good, and pleases God our Savior, who wants all men to be saved and to come to a knowledge of the truth" (1 Tim. 2:24). In an orderly society, in the peace and quiet of life, the gospel can spread and people can be won for Christ. And this agrees with God's desire for the salvation of humanity.

Nobody knows the date of Christ's return. Nobody knows why it takes so long. The only sense we have found in the continuation of history and the "not yet" of Christ's return is God's compassion and our mission.

The Last Judgment, detail

—Fra Angelico, 1400-1455

CHAPTER 3

ENGAGED IN THE MISSION OF THE LAST DAYS

The work of Christ at his first coming constitutes the beginning of the end (ch. 1). What he began will be finished. The Scriptures say that his second coming is soon and certain. The only uncertainty is our ability to hold out till he comes (ch. 2). The best way to prepare for Christ's coming is to play our part in God's mission for these last days.

The Interim

By choosing twelve apostles, Jesus began to gather the remnant of the twelve tribes of Israel. He trained his followers to be a new community that would practice the love of our Father in heaven (Matt. 5:43-48), oppose worldly values, honor children, and prize servanthood (Matt. 20:25-27). Christ appointed the disciples to be the salt of the earth and the light of the world, and thus to be witnesses to the goodness of God (Matt. 5:13-16), which was Israel's original assignment. He promised them great honor in God's future when all of God's people would be gathered again (Matt. 19:28).

During the interim period between the resurrection and the return of their Master, the people of the Messiah have to fulfill a mission for the kingdom of God. The "sending of the twelve" is the first preliminary action or exercise (Matt. 10; Mark 6:8-12; Luke 9:1-6—see also Luke 10, the sending of the seventy-two). When Jesus sends his followers to announce the kingdom, he gives his "mission speech" (esp. Matt. 10). Some features of that speech apply only to that first, historic mission. The disciples must bring the message of the kingdom in word and deed without carrying any money or extra clothes with them. "Do not take along any gold or silver or copper in your belts; take no bag for the journey, or extra tunic, or sandals or a staff; for the worker is worth his keep" (Matt. 10:9-10). They must rely on the hospitality of those who believe the message. However, this carefree behavior is not for all times and places. Later Jesus himself says: "But now, if you have a purse, take it, and also a bag; and if you don't have a sword, sell your cloak and buy one" (Luke 22:36). Missionaries should make appropriate preparations for perilous times.

Also Jesus' command to the twelve not to go to the Gentiles—"Go rather to the lost sheep of Israel" (Matt. 10:6)—is no longer valid, although the gospel of the kingdom is still always "first for the Jew, then for the Gentile" (Rom. 1:16).

At the same time, this speech of Jesus, like all his end-time speeches, has a far wider scope than this first skirmish between the kingdom of heaven and the kingdom of the devil. Prophetically Jesus speaks of all the tribulations through which the people of the Messiah will have to go when fulfilling their assignment. "On my account you will be brought before governors and kings as witnesses to them and to the Gentiles" (Matt. 10:18). That's how Jesus envisions the mission after Pentecost—it will be "to the Gentiles" as well. In this speech Jesus also calms our fears. Three times he says, "Don't be afraid" (vv. 26-31). He knows that what keeps most of us from faithful performance of our mission is fear of people.

At that point, Jesus speaks a very remarkable word in connection with the mission of his followers: "I tell you the truth, you will not finish going through the cities of Israel before the Son of Man comes" (Matt. 10:23). This saying has troubled interpreters for ages, and it has led some to say that Jesus erred when he predicted his early coming in glory (see ch. 2). It is one of those prophetic utterances that speaks of an event far in the future but that is pictured in the local time and place. Jesus was speaking about the persecution his followers must endure during the time between his departure and his return. He encourages them. He assures them there will always be a place of refuge. Before they run out of places, "the Son of Man comes." When he does, our mission will be accomplished.

Stewards

Jesus uses the idea of stewardship to explain what his disciples must do and how they should live during the interim. In Bible times, travel was slow. When people went on a journey, they would entrust their house or business to *stewards,* trusted slaves, family members, or friends. A steward did the work of a trustee. The steward had full authority to transact business and to rule the household until the master returned. The master's return was also the day of reckoning. Since the master's trip was not scheduled by a travel agency, the steward would not know when that day would be.

The most desirable trait of such a steward is faithfulness. A faithful steward will always think of his master. Every night the books and the business are organized in such a way that the steward is ready to give an account, should the master come home during the night.

So Jesus urged, "Be on guard! Be alert! You do not know when that time will come. It's like a man going away: He leaves his house and puts his servants in charge, each with his assigned task, and tells the one at the door to keep watch" (Mark 13:33-34).

In Matthew 24:45-46 Jesus asks, "Who then is the faithful and wise servant, whom the master has put in charge of the servants in his household to give them their food at the proper time? It will be good for that servant whose master finds him doing so when he returns."

"Again, [the kingdom of heaven] will be like a man going on a journey, who called his servants and entrusted his property to them. To one he gave five talents of money, to another two talents and to another one talent . . ." (Matt. 25:14-15).

In this last parable (Matt. 25:14-30), each servant becomes a trustee. The trustees must show their loyalty to their master by their work during his absence. The master punishes the servant who hid the money in the ground, because the servant refused to work and to take the necessary risks. This warns us that the church that does not go to work and avoids taking risks in doing the business of the Master will be punished.

The passages in Matthew that refer to the church (Matt. 16:17-19; 18:15-20) are also based on the idea of stewardship during the interim. Jesus entrusts "the keys of the kingdom of heaven" to Peter (Matt. 16:19). And he gives the power of the keys, the authority to "bind and to loose," to the church (Matt. 18:17-18). In John 20:22-23, he gives that power to the apostles. The trustees receive the keys. They are empowered to take care of the Master's household during his absence.

The Activity of the Spirit

We are now living in "the last days." That is the biblical term for the period of time between Christ's ascension and his return (Acts 2:17; Heb. 1:2). The great gift of the last days is the Holy Spirit. The Spirit's coming is the sign that the last days have begun (Joel 2:28; Ezek. 37).

The Holy Spirit lives in God's people, who together form God's temple (1 Cor. 3:16; Eph. 2:22; 1 Pet. 2:4-5). We are God's dwelling place in the present world.

The Spirit of God equips God's people to fulfil their mission. He enables us to endure the temptations and persecutions that are also a feature of the last days, and he makes us victorious.

The gifts of the Spirit provide the spiritual power for the church's life and mission. We have three lists of these gifts in the New Testament: Romans 12:6-8; 1 Corinthians 12; and Ephesians 4:11 (but see also 1 Pet. 4:10-11). We should not read these lists as if they are an exact and exhaustive inventory of the Spirit's gifts in the early church. The Lord distributes the Spirit's special gifts (*charismata*) according to the need of the hour, according to the prayers of Christians, and according to his sovereign pleasure. However, all Christians receive the three general gifts of the Spirit for our life and our mission: faith, hope, and love. The greatest of these is love (1 Cor. 13:13; Col. 1:4-5). Christian love is also the standard by which we must measure the usefulness of all other gifts (1 Cor. 13).

The presence of the Holy Spirit in our lives also provides the connection with the life to come. When we "have shared in the Holy Spirit," then we "have tasted the goodness of the word of God and the powers of the coming age . . . " (Heb. 6:4-5). By having the Holy Spirit here and now, we have a down payment of all the goodness and riches of the future (Eph. 1:14).

The resurrected Jesus is the firstfruits of redeemed humanity now with God in heaven. The Spirit is the firstfruits of the world to come, now present with us on earth (1 Cor. 15:23; Rom. 8:23).

In these last days, we are engaged in God's mission, knowing that it cannot last long anymore. We sense that the end is near, not because we know God's calendar, but because of the great things that have happened already. Our human nature is in heaven and God's Spirit is already on earth. The rings have been exchanged. Pledge and counterpledge have been made. Heaven and earth must soon be reunited. Soon we will be together with God forever (Rev. 21:3-4).

Our life in Christ—that is to say, our lives as far as they are now governed and sanctified by the Spirit of God—will never pass away. They constitute the beginning of the future state. The new age and the future life have already begun in the present world, for Christian love never ceases. And the new heaven, the new earth, and our new bodies will be created by the Holy Spirit, who already lives in ordinary believers.

Describing Christ's Return

The early Christians did not speak of Christ's *second coming* but simply of his *coming*. The word "coming," *parousia* in the original Greek, is never used for what we call the first coming of Jesus. The only *parousia* is the one we are now expecting. That does not prevent us from speaking of a first and second coming, as some do—after all, the Bible *does* speak of a *second time:* "he will appear a second time, not to bear sin, but to bring salvation to those who are waiting for him" (Heb. 9:28). Nevertheless, it's significant that the church used to speak of only one *parousia,* one coming of Jesus, and that Jesus was for them the coming One.

Early Christians also spoke of the "appearance" (Greek: *epiphaneia)* of Jesus: "Keep this command without spot or blame until the appearing of our Lord Jesus Christ" (1 Tim. 6:14). When we say we expect the appearance of Jesus, we imply that he is not visible at the present time. He has disappeared from our sight.

Another expression the early church used for the coming of Christ is "revelation" (Greek: *apokalupsis*), as in: "you eagerly wait for our Lord Jesus Christ to be revealed" (1 Cor. 1:7). In Colossians 3:4 Paul writes, "When Christ, who is your life is revealed, then you also will be revealed with him in glory" (NRSV). Elsewhere the Bible can say that Jesus reveals some *thing* (Rev. 1:2), but here it speaks of the revelation of Christ himself. This means that he is hidden at the present time. He is here, but he is veiled, and so is his glory. When his glory is unveiled, ours will be evident too.

The Day

Most frequently, however, the early Christians would speak of "the day," just as the Old Testament spoke of "the day of the Lord." In the Old Testament "the day of the Lord" was the day when God would arise and set things straight in the present world. The prophets had warned that it would be a dreadful day, a day of judgment (Joel 2:31, quoted in Acts 2:20). In the New Testament that day belongs to the Lord Jesus.

In the gospels Jesus speaks of "the day of the Son of Man." It will be the day of final judgment, when the Son of Man will be the judge. Jesus always called himself "the Son of Man," in part to hide his identity, since I too am a son of man, and you are a son or a daughter of man as well. But when Jesus called himself *the* Son of Man (not just *a* son of man), he was also claiming to be the figure of Daniel 7. He is the One who will come with the clouds of heaven (Dan. 7:13; Matt. 26:64). To this Jesus, the Son of Man, God has given "everlasting dominion that will not pass away, and his kingdom is one that will never be destroyed" (Dan. 7:14).

"The day of the Son of Man" is the last day, judgment day. It's the day on which it will become crystal clear to everybody who Jesus is. But it will be too late for many. Therefore we must now be loyal to him, remain alert, and pray to escape the temptations of these present days, so that we will "be able to stand before the Son of Man" (Luke 21:36), salute the conqueror, and report, "Mission accomplished."

Sometimes the New Testament simply speaks of "the day" (1 Thess. 5:4; 1 Cor. 3:13), and everyone understands that it's the day when Jesus will come. "Because I know whom I have believed, and am convinced that he is able to guard what I have entrusted to him for that day" (2 Tim. 1:12). "That day" is the day of judgment and the day when all who long for his appearance receive the crown of righteousness (2 Tim. 4:8). What the Old Testament prophets called the day of the Lord is now "the day of Christ Jesus" or the "day of Christ" (Phil. 1:6, 10; 2:16).

Sudden as a Robbery

The coming of the Lord will come as a surprise. It will be unexpected. Jesus himself must have been the first one to compare the event with a burglary: "If the owner of the house had known at what time of night the thief was coming, he would have kept watch . . . " (Matt. 24:43; see also Luke 12:39).

This comparison is not between Jesus and a thief, as if the two had anything in common. But the return of Christ is an event for which we cannot mark the calendar, just as we cannot set the clock for the time a robber strikes.

Apparently this saying became very popular among Jesus' followers. We find it in the literature of Paul, Peter, and John. Paul writes, "The day of the Lord will come like a thief in the night" (1 Thess. 5:2). But we don't fear its coming, because we are already living as "sons [and daughters] of the day" (5:5); we have already gone from the darkness of sin to the light of God's salvation.

Peter also warns us that "the day of the Lord will come like a thief" (2 Pet. 3:10). In both cases the day's coming is compared with the stealth of a thief. That's no different than "the coming of the Lord," except that "the day" carries with it the notion of judgment on the wicked.

In Revelation 3:3 Jesus warns the church of Sardis, "If you do not wake up, I will come like a thief, and you will not know at what time I will come to you." This too refers to a coming in judgment. Here we do not need to think of the last judgment. The final judgment is not the only judgment that suddenly comes upon the unrepentant.

In Revelation 16:15, in the midst of scenes of awful judgment, the voice of Jesus cries, "Behold, I come like a thief! Blessed is he who stays awake. . . . "

The day of the Lord cannot be pinpointed. The judgment will suddenly fall on wicked, unsuspecting people. That's why the Christian church incorporated the sayings about Jesus' "coming like a thief" in her vocabulary. The church of Christ stays alert and awake while it warns the whole world that judgment is approaching.

The Day of Grace Is Ending

Today is the interim: the time between the ascension and the return of Christ. This is the gospel era, the time in which the good news must be proclaimed to the whole world and applied to all aspects of life.

Through the prophet Isaiah, God promised that "in the time of my favor I will answer you, and in the day of salvation I will help you" (Isa. 49:8). The whole prophecy of Isaiah 49:8ff. is framed in terms of the Year of Jubilee and a restoration of Israel. Paul proclaims that Isaiah's prediction is fulfilled today: "I tell you now is the time of God's favor, now is the day of salvation" (2 Cor. 6:2).

This "day of salvation," just as "the last days," stands for the period between the first and the second coming of the Lord. During this period of grace it holds true that "everyone who calls on the name of the LORD will be saved" (Joel 2:32; Acts 2:21; Rom. 10:13). But people must call now, otherwise it will be too late. Because the church of Christ remembers her Master's sayings about the thief-like coming of the end, we have been singing a missionary song since the days of Paul:

> Wake up, O sleeper,
> rise from the dead,
> and Christ will shine on you.
> —Ephesians 5:14

The knowledge of the approaching end and the coming judgment adds an edge of urgency to the missionary calling of the church. The Bible knows nothing of second or third chances. But those who believe in a "rapture" and a "millennium" believe there will be new "ages" and new chances for salvation. I will discuss these later.

This is the day of salvation. Today God's grace is extended to the whole world. During this time period all people ought to be confronted with the love of God in Christ Jesus. Today God "commands all people everywhere to repent. For he has set a day when he will judge the world with justice by the man he has appointed" (Acts 17:30-31). That man is Jesus. After this day of salvation comes the day of wrath.

Signs of Christ's Coming

As I said above, the New Testament speaks of the coming of Jesus as imminent (anytime soon), as dependent on certain conditions (only after this and that has happened), and as an unknown date, which no one can calculate because even Jesus does not know it. These three strands are present in the gospels and in the letters of Paul and Peter. Apparently the earliest writers and readers felt no need to reconcile them.

Far too many people attempt to make up a schedule of coming events on the basis of the signs of Christ's coming. They mainly gather these "signs of his coming" from the one eschatological speech of Jesus (Matt. 24; Mark 13; Luke 21) and from Paul's second letter to the Thessalonians. There Paul explains that first the man of sin must be revealed before the Lord will come.

In Mark 13 and its parallels, Jesus answers the questions of his disciples as to when the temple would be destroyed and what the sign would be of Christ's "coming and of the end of the age" (Matt. 24:3). Jesus answers them in a prophetic speech, which has as its central historical prediction the destruction of Jerusalem and of the temple. In Matthew and Mark, Jesus describes the end of the world and the coming of the Son of Man as an extension of the national crisis of that time. He speaks in a way similar to the way in which Old Testament prophecies describe the future in local color.

This end-time speech of Jesus, usually called the Olivet discourse, is enormously valuable for us. His promise of the end is sealed in the prediction of the fate of the temple. The destruction of Jerusalem in A.D. 70 says loudly and clearly that whatever Christ said about the great future is reliable. Jesus can be trusted.

The Olivet discourse is also deeply disturbing. Christ certainly did not promise his followers a happy and quiet life: wars, rumors of wars, earthquakes, famines—and those are only the beginning of the woes. That's the panorama of human history and a sign that the end is coming. As for the church of Christ, it will face the temptations of the pseudo-Christs and the hatred of the true Christ. It will experience tribulations and persecutions until the very end. However, this discourse of Jesus gives no signs by which the end can be calculated.

The tenor of the Olivet discourse is no different from all the other exhortations Jesus addressed to the church in the interim. He tells them not to worry when facing the worldly judges; they should rely on the Holy Spirit (Mark 13:11). "He who stands firm to the end will be saved" (v. 13). "False Christs . . . will appear . . . so be on your guard" (vv. 22-23). And just as you can see that spring is coming and summer is approaching when you look at trees, so you know that the Son of Man is coming when you see wars and earthquakes, the destruction of Jerusalem, signs in heaven and signs on earth (v. 29). "What I say to you, I say to everyone: 'Watch!'" (v. 37).

There are two kinds of road signs. One kind warns the driver about curves, bumps, intersections, construction, and obstructions. These signs are designed to keep us alert and cautious while we travel. The other signs tell us how far we have to travel to the next town: Washington 150 (mi.), Ottawa 200 (km.).

The signs that Jesus gives us keep his followers alert, cautious, and confident. However, some people read these signs as if they tell us how close we are to our destination. These fellow Christians are always calculating. And in every generation they try to correct the mistakes of the previous generation, recalculating the miles we still have to travel. We'll discuss some of their calendars and calculations in the next chapter. But it doesn't work that way. The signs do not tell us *when* Jesus is coming but *that* he is coming.

Between D-Day and V-Day

Perhaps Oscar Cullmann was the first one to use the following example (*Christ and Time*, p. 84). To me, it has been one of the most helpful ways of thinking about the time in which we are living, mainly because I lived through the dark time between D-Day and V-Day during World War II. In June 1944 the Allied forces landed on the beaches of Normandy, France. That was D-Day. At great cost, they knocked a hole in Hitler's "Atlantic Wall" and began their march to Berlin and the heart of Europe. We knew that the decisive battle had been won. On D-Day the outcome of the war was decided. Then there were days and weeks when we thought the war was just about over. We could not believe the Nazis might go on for more than a month. And yet the war lasted another eleven months. During those long, dark months, we who lived in Nazi-occupied territory suffered more than ever before. On May 5, 1945, we were free at last. That was V-Day, Victory Day.

When this world was invaded by the Son of God, when he died to remove the curse and rose to make a new beginning, we knew that the decisive battle had been won. And many thought and said that the war would be over soon, very soon. Christ's first coming was D-Day. Now V-Day is sure to come, but we don't know when. And just as we had to go through a dark, fearful, and painful period before victory could be celebrated at the end of World War II, so Christians may have to go through many months of testing until, at last, all flags are flying, all tumult has ended, and true shalom is here.

Today it is not important that we know how long this period between D-Day and V-Day is going to last. Of the utmost importance is what we do while it lasts.

The Garden of Earthly Delights: Triptych, hell detail

—Hieronymus Bosch, 1450-1516

CHAPTER 4

CALENDARS AND CALCULATORS

We don't know the date of "the day." And we aren't supposed to know it. The sayings of Jesus are quite clear on that point.

- "No one knows about that day or hour, not even the angels in heaven, nor the Son, but only the Father" (Matt. 24:36).

- "It is not for you to know the times or dates the Father has set by his own authority" (Acts 1:7).

Nevertheless, there have always been Christians who tried to figure out when Jesus would come back. Usually these forecasters discovered God's timeline in parts of the Bible that many Christians consider obscure, such as parts of Daniel, Ezekiel, and Revelation. What follows is an illustration of the fact that this bad practice of calculation has gone on throughout church history.

In the Early Church

The prophet Montanus and the prophetesses Priscilla and Maximilla were the leaders of a movement in Phrygia (Asia Minor) around A.D. 170. In church history books the movement is called *Montanism.* These people renounced earthly leisure and luxury and announced the Lord's imminent return. Maximilla died in 179, but was remembered for her words: "After me shall be no prophetess any more, but the consummation" (J. D. Douglas, ed., *The New International Dictionary of the Christian Church,* p. 644).

End-time expectation and date-setting for the coming of the Lord have existed since the earliest times, but usually on the fringes of the church. Churchmen like Origen in the third century and Augustine in the fifth set the standard for orthodoxy.

During the Middle Ages

The crusades were fueled by apocalyptic visions. Western European knights and soldiers went on a mission for God. They would liberate Jerusalem and defeat the anti-Christian Jew and Muslim. The religious teachers in Western Europe promised forgiveness and everlasting glory to those who would kill and be killed in this holy war. Onward Christian soldiers.

The prophecy expert of those days, Joachim of Fiore (who died in approximately 1202), was a dispensationalist of sorts. He wrote a commentary on the Apocalypse, the book of Revelation, and he had as many charts and timelines as modern-day prophecy pundits. But for him, the good Christians were in Western Europe and the Antichrist was a Jew. In today's line-up for the last days, according to modern pundits, God's children are *the Jews* and the Antichrist comes from *Western Europe*. Joachim sowed the seeds of anti-Semitism, which bore bitter fruits in Europe. Anti-Semitism in those days was not merely hostility towards Jews, which is today's meaning, but hatred towards both Jews and Muslims, the children of Isaac and Ishmael.

In the Sixteenth Century

During Reformation times it was the Anabaptists who expected the imminent return of the Lord. "All Anabaptists were united in their conviction that the return of Christ was near" and that "Christ and Antichrist were locked in their final struggle," observes Walter Klassen, historian of the Mennonites (quoted by Paul Boyer, *When Time Shall Be No More,* p. 59).

The revolutionary wing of the otherwise peaceful Anabaptists did not only expect Jesus Christ to come and rescue the oppressed, but believed they aided him greatly with a radical overhaul of the existing order. The Anabaptist preacher of Muenster, Germany, came to the conviction that God had chosen his city as the New Jerusalem. Radicals flocked to the town. Jan Mathys, a baker from Haarlem, the Netherlands, took charge, together with another Dutchman, Jan Beukelssen, a tailor from Leyden. The city was surrounded by Roman Catholic and Lutheran armies. The baker was killed in a sortie and John of Leyden was proclaimed king of Muenster. "Polygamy was established, community of goods was enforced, opponents were slaughtered" (W. Walker, *A History of the Christian Church,* p. 459). Finally, in June 1535, the city was captured. The surviving leaders were tortured until they died.

The radicalism of Anabaptist millennialists had a strong negative influence on Calvin ("frenzied devils" he called them), on Luther, who wrote "against the murdering and robbing hordes of peasants" (Paul Boyer, *When Time Shall Be No More,* p. 60), and on Zwingli, who did not protest when Zurich's civil authorities drowned an Anabaptist leader.

Reformed confessions still echo abhorrence of "Anabaptists and other anarchists" (Belgic Confession, Art. 36). And the (Lutheran) Augsburg Confession denounces the Jewish dreams of the Anabaptists' millennialism.

Zwingli dismissed Revelation as "not a Book of the Bible." For a while, at least, Luther considered the last Bible book as "neither apostolic nor prophetic," and Calvin did not lecture or write a commentary on it. That does not mean that the Reformers did not speak often about the return of the Lord—they did. They also knew who the Antichrist was—the pope, of course. But the Reformed and Lutheran traditions have retained a strong suspicion of end-time speculation since Reformation days. The behavior of revolutionary Anabaptists might well be a reason for their caution.

Recent Predictions and Disappointments

William Miller (1782-1849) was a Baptist farmer in upstate New York who proclaimed that Jesus would return "about the year 1843." The date he derived from Daniel 8:14: "It will take 2,300 evenings and mornings; then the sanctuary will be reconsecrated." Miller gained tens of thousands of followers called "Millerites." When 1843 came and went, the date was reset for October 22, 1844. That became the day of "the Disappointment," as it's called in Seventh-Day Adventist literature. "From the peak of anticipation, Millerites were cast into the deepest gloom. There were serious problems for those who had given up all their possessions. Their businesses abandoned, their crops ungathered, they were confused and many were in want" (Godfrey T. Anderson, "The Great Second Advent Awakening to 1844" in *The Advent Hope in Scripture and History*, p. 169).

Out of the Millerite excitement grew the Seventh-Day Adventist Church. Other organizations of Adventists have also persisted to this day. One outgrowth was the Watchtower Bible and Tract Society (Jehovah's Witnesses) founded in 1844 by Charles Taze Russell. Russell's system, based on his calculations from Daniel and the book of Revelation, has numerous points of contact with contemporary premillennialist and dispensational teachings. But these do not share the Jehovah's Witnesses' heresy about Jesus Christ as a higher creature or a lesser God. Russell predicted the end of the present world in 1914. Later presidents of the Jehovah's Witnesses, such as Rutherford and Knorr, set dates for 1925 and 1975.

It's one of the riddles of religious history that followers continue to honor leaders even after the leaders turn out to be false prophets.

The Bad Practice Continues

Former NASA scientist Edgar Whisenant wrote the two-million-copy best-seller *88 Reasons Why the Rapture Will Be in 1988*. The "rapture" would take place between September 11 and 13, 1988. World War III would start in October. Then he wrote *The Final Shout: Rapture Report 1989,* stating that he had forgotten that the first century had only ninety-nine years, so the rapture would be a year later, in 1989.

On October 29, 1992, twenty thousand Koreans waited until midnight for the rapture to occur. They gathered in the Church of the Coming Days in Seoul and in two hundred other congregations in South Korea. After that date, their prophet, Lee Jang-rim, remained in prison, charged with swindling the believers out of four million dollars.

Harold Camping was a prominent member of the Christian Reformed Church until 1988. He calculated that Jesus would come back in September 1994. He wrote two books to warn the world: *1994?* and *Are You Ready?* If you were to tell Harold Camping that nobody, not even Jesus, knows about that day or hour (Matt. 24:36), he would say: "True, we don't know the day, or the time of day, but we can know the year and the month." Harold Camping thought he was not in conflict with Christ's sayings in Matthew 24:36 and Acts 1:7 when he predicted the Lord would return in September 1994. It's hard to argue with such people.

Dispensationalism Sets the Tone

Premilliennialism is the belief that Christ's return will precede and bring about a thousand-year rule of Jesus on earth. The father of the North American brand of premillennialism was John Nelson Darby (1800-1882), an Irish clergyman and one of the early leaders of the so-called Plymouth Brethren. You may never have heard of him, but you cannot listen to North American religious television or browse in any evangelical bookstore without meeting his disciples.

Darby visited North America and influenced, among many others, evangelist Dwight L. Moody. Moody Bible Institute in Chicago has remained an ardent defender of premillennial belief. But Darby's heaviest impact in North America came through Cyrus I. Scofield, who made Darby's view of prophecy an integral part of the notes he included in the *Scofield Reference Bible*, King James Version. The first edition was published in 1909. Millions of copies of the *Scofield Reference Bible* have been sold and studied since that time. In 1967 a committee prepared a revised edition, the *New Scofield Reference Bible*. In 1989 this Bible appeared with the text of the New King James Version. This is now *the* Bible for the premillennial dispensationalists (dispensationalists are Christians who believe that God works very differently in each stage, or dispensation, of salvation history).

As for Scofield's notes, he may be wrong sometimes, but he is never in doubt. That's also a feature of his followers. The absolute certainty of these prophecy interpreters bowls over a large audience.

Dispensational premillennialism has been promoted especially by Dallas Theological Seminary and its graduates. Lewis Sperry Chafer, the first president of Dallas Seminary (1924-1952), and John F. Walvoort, its second president (1952-1986), are well-known authors in the Darby-Scofield tradition, as are two other Dallas professors, Charles C. Ryrie and J. Dwight Pentecost. Dallas supplies the theologians for the movement. But the popular spread of this particular brand of North American evangelical faith happened, and still happens, through Bible schools, prophecy conferences, paperbacks, and videotapes. By these means the teachers present their charts of God's programs, based on Daniel, Ezekiel, Zechariah, and Revelation. They mark the comings (plural!) of the Lord, the different resurrections of the dead, the five judgments, and the seven dispensations. And they teach that the time of the rapture of the true church is very close.

The Darby-Scofield system is the theological background of most evangelical preachers who crowd our airwaves. As long as they extol Christ and preach the gospel, we are grateful for them. When they give their commentary on world problems in the light of "what must happen according to Bible prophecy," they are an embarrassment to the Christian church.

Today's Prophecy Prediction Preachers

All people have an innate curiosity about the future. It's a trait that has always made people pay for clairvoyants, palm readers, psychics, and astrologers. Christians in the Darby-Scofield tradition consider the study of Bible prophecy the religious counterpart of secular fortune-telling. Later on, in chapter 10, we'll see that theirs is really an *abuse* of biblical prophecy.

No writer for the prophecy-prediction line has been more successful than Hal Lindsey. His book *The Late Great Planet Earth* was published in 1970. The book broke many records but no new ground. It is a popular, journalistic version of what he learned at Dallas Seminary. In 1996 Zondervan reported that eleven million copies of the book are in print. In addition, the commercial spin-off of *The Late Great Planet Earth* includes study guides, picture books by Spire Christian Comics, and films. The book has been translated into many languages.

Lindsey, writing with Carole C. Carlson, very deliberately set out to offer the biblical prophets as the most reliable foretellers of the future. Compared with Jeanne Dixon, the track record of Isaiah shows pinpoint accuracy, he said. Already three hundred specific predictions have been fulfilled and the others are about to become reality. For this reason, Lindsey urged his readers to forsake astrology and to pick up the Bible.

But in Lindsey's book the focus of the Bible has changed. God, who spoke in the Old Testament through prophets and seers, and who in these last days spoke to us by his Son (Heb. 1:1), is not saying much through the Son in Lindsey's book. In *The Late Great Planet Earth,* the appearance of the Son of God in the flesh serves no other purpose than to prove that the prophets are reliable fortune-tellers. And Lindsey knows exactly what the prophetic program is for the bloody finale of our planet's history.

Lindsey, and the hundreds of authors who tried to write a bestseller after him, are dispensationalists à la Scofield and Darby. When it comes to the discussions of the end, they have managed to take center stage in North America. The rest of us must react to what they have been saying. So before I present what they call "God's program for the last days," we should concentrate on some basic teachings and flaws of premillennial dispensationalism.

Some Basic Teachings of Dispensationalism

Dispensationalists teach that the history of God's dealings with humanity can be divided into seven time periods. The people living during each of these dispensations are tested by a different principle. Briefly stated, the dispensations are the following:

- Innocence—Paradise

- Conscience—the Fall to the Flood

- Human Government—Noah to Babel

- Promise—Abraham to Egypt

- Law—Moses to John the Baptist

- Grace—the Church Age

- Kingdom—the Millennium

However, this sevenfold division of history no longer constitutes an important issue for debate among Christians. Even the contrast between the Mosaic period as a dispensation of "law" and the gospel age as a time of "grace" is no longer a real problem between dispensational and non-dispensational Christians. At one time it was a problem. However, the 1967 edition of the *Scofield Reference Bible* teaches that "a recognition of the dispensations is of highest value, so long as it is clearly understood that throughout all the Scriptures there is only one basis of salvation, that is, by grace through faith" (*New Scofield Study Bible*, p. xi).

So what remains as the distinctive teaching of dispensationalism? "The essence of dispensationalism is the distinction between Israel and the Church" (Charles C. Ryrie, *Dispensationalism Today*, p. 47).

The chief dogma of dispensationalism is "that there are two people of God for whom God has two different programs and destinies—theocratic and earthly for Israel, spiritual and heavenly for the Church" (George E. Ladd, *The Last Things*, p. 9).

God's old covenant promises to Abraham and David are *not* fulfilled in the New Testament age, they claim. As a matter of fact, the Old Testament does not know anything about the church age. "[T]he present age is a parenthesis or a time period not predicted by the Old Testament and therefore not fulfilling or advancing the program of events revealed in the Old Testament foreview" (John F. Walvoord, *The Millennial Kingdom*, p. 231). The church as the body of Christ in which Jews and Gentiles are united on a basis of equality is a "mystery" that was "not made known" and "hid in God" until it was revealed through the apostle Paul (Walvoord, p. 232-237). "Of importance to premillennialism is the obvious conclusion that if God's present dealings with the body of Christ do not fulfill his promises concerning the Kingdom Age then a future fulfillment is demanded" (p. 237).

He means that a literal fulfillment of the promises will take place when Israel is restored to God, exalted above all nations, when Christ rules over them for a thousand years in the city of Jerusalem.

Those of us who are unfamiliar with the premillennial dispensationalist way of Bible reading are taken aback to hear that the New did not fulfill the Old. We will object: But didn't Mary, Zacharias, and Simeon praise God for fulfilling the promises made to Abraham and David (Luke 1-2)? Didn't John and Jesus announce the kingdom of God? Didn't Jesus himself say that the Father had sent him to "preach the good news of the kingdom of God" (Luke 4:43)?

Their answer is that Jesus offered the kingdom to Israel but the leaders of Israel rejected his offer. The leadership committed the unpardonable sin by saying that Christ did his mighty works by the power of Beelzebub, the prince of demons (Matt. 12:22-32). After that a new program began. Jesus turned to those who were his spiritual relatives: "Here are my mother and my brothers" (Matt. 12:49).

Instead of offering the Davidic, earthly kingdom to Israel, he began to teach a secret kingdom (see the parable of the seed, Matt. 13), laying the basis for the church age. Ultimately the rejected King was crucified. For further descriptions of these teachings, see the *New Scofield Study Bible* on Matthew 4:17; 12:3, 18, 46; 21:4; J. Dwight Pentecost, *Thy Kingdom Come*, chapter 18; and Lewis Sperry Chafer, *Systematic Theology*, Abridged Edition, p. 366.

Dispensationalists teach that the promise of the restoration of David's kingdom was not fulfilled when Christ died for us, but will only be fulfilled when he comes again to set up the millennial kingdom of Israel. Charles C. Ryrie states it tersely: "A lot of confusion would be avoided if we would remember a very simple comparison: the first coming of Christ was related to the cross, the second to the kingdom" (*The Final Countdown*, p. 23). So premillennial dispensationalists have the gospel and they have the kingdom. But they do not have the gospel *of* the kingdom.

I will deal with some of the dispensationalist assumptions, such as the millennium and the relationship of Israel and the church, in later chapters.

As for the "rejection and postponement" of the kingdom of David, this teaching always makes us ask: If the Jews had accepted the kingdom, would there have been any place, any necessity for the cross? (Oswald T. Allis, *Prophecy and the Church*, p. 75). Charles Ryrie tackled the question "Is the Cross Minimized" in his book *Dispensationalism Today* (pp. 161-168). Of course, he claims that premillennialists do not downplay but actually magnify the cross. "The crucifixion was as necessary to the establishing of the kingdom as it was to the building of the Church" (*Dispensationalism Today*, p. 165). That's good to hear. Usually the premils present the arrival of the millennial kingdom in terms of a militant Messiah, one who is unlike the Jesus of the gospels. He is victorious in the Battle of Armageddon, and then he establishes his rule over the world from his headquarters in Jerusalem. However, Ryrie and his colleagues don't help us understand *how* the cross of Jesus relates to the earthly Jewish kingdom they expect.

In the last fifteen years or so, younger scholarly dispensationalists have been writing about the relationship between Israel and the church. They call themselves "progressive dispensationalists." They do not deny that much Old Testament prophecy is fulfilled in the church. However, their influence is not yet evident on a popular level. Stanley J. Grenz of Regent College, Vancouver, British Columbia, has high hopes for what has begun in scholarly circles at Dallas Theological Seminary. "As progressive dispensationalists continue to grapple with the central problem of the relationship of Israel to the church, they constitute perhaps the most significant development in the larger dispensationalist movement . . . with this more cautious dispensationalism lies the future of the movement and its ongoing contribution to evangelical theology" (*The Millennial Maze*, p. 125). Let's hope he's right.

Meanwhile, let's look at the calendar of future events that our dispensationalist friends confidently present as God's agenda.

God's Blueprint

God's Blueprint for Future Events is the subtitle of a small book by Charles C. Ryrie titled *The Final Countdown*. It is amazing how Ryrie and his friends can read "God's blueprint" so clearly where all angels and prophets need glasses, so to speak, and all ordinary believers are stunned. But it is this dogmatic certainty that is the secret for the popularity of the Darby-Scofield system.

When they draw the timeline for God's future acts, the dispensational pre-mils start with Daniel. King Nebuchadnezzar's dream, recounted in Daniel 2, gives the first clue. The statue showed four empires of decreasing glory. During the time of the fourth empire, the Roman empire, the kingdom of God would be set up. All of us know that the Messiah was born when the Roman emperor "Caesar Augustus issued a decree that a census should be taken of the entire Roman world" (Luke 2:1). And all of us would say that Daniel was speaking of the coming of Jesus. The birth of the Baby means that the peace of heaven came to earth. It's the time of the setting up of the kingdom of heaven. But the dis-pensationalist would disagree. Ryrie writes, "Obviously, at His first coming Christ did not even establish a kingdom in Palestine, to say nothing of the whole earth. Therefore we are forced to conclude that the kingdom will be set up at His Second Coming" (*The Final Countdown,* p. 23).

So the setting up of the kingdom for Israel takes place when Jesus returns to sit on his throne in Jerusalem. That's made "clear" with the help of Daniel 7. The fourth beast, corresponding to the fourth empire of Daniel 2, has ten horns, just like the image in Daniel 2 had ten toes. These stand for ten kings who will arise out of the fourth—the Roman—empire. It seems to be a bit of a jump to go from ten emperors of Rome to a federation of ten European coun-tries and the present effort for achieving European economic unity. But that's exactly what the prophecy interpreters tell us. The European nations will com-bine to form a ten-nation federacy, the revived Roman Empire.

Most of the prophecy pundits say that the contemporary European Union is the link with the coming evil federation. And the little horn that will "subdue three kings" and "speak against the Most High and oppress his saints" (7:8, 24-25) is the Antichrist. He will be the leader in Europe, probably Rome. Three of the nations will not join him willingly. He will force them into submission. The other seven will join him voluntarily. So the beast, the Antichrist, the "Future Führer," as Hal Lindsey calls him, has ten horns but seven heads (Rev. 13:1). And this revived Roman emperor will be used by Satan to do miraculous things. He will be the world ruler and all people will worship him. "The saints will be handed over to him for a time, times and half a time" (Dan. 7:25). That means, according to the dispensationalists, that for one-half of seven years (1+2+½) he will oppress, persecute, and kill the Jewish nation.

The Seven Years

The prophecy students in the Darby-Scofield tradition are unanimous in teaching a seven-year period of unprecedented tribulation. They speak often and very dogmatically about these seven years. They even write grotesque nov-els that play out during this seven-year period. Therefore, one would assume that the seven years are clearly taught in Scripture. Actually, they find the number seven in a debatable but ingenious understanding of Daniel 9:27. Once they have the seven, they pour all the suffering that Jesus announced in his speeches

In Daniel 9, the angel Gabriel gives God's answer to Daniel's prayer for the redemption of Israel:

24"Seventy 'sevens' [or 'weeks'] are decreed for your people and your holy city to finish transgression, to put an end to sin, to atone for wickedness, to bring in everlasting righteousness, to seal up vision and prophecy and to anoint the most holy [this anointing may refer to a place or a person]. 25Know and understand this: From the issuing of the decree to restore and rebuild Jerusalem until the [or "an"] Anointed One, the ruler, comes, there will be seven 'sevens' and sixty-two 'sevens.' It will be rebuilt with streets and a trench, but in times of trouble. 26After the sixty-two 'sevens' the Anointed One will be cut off and will have nothing. The people of the ruler who will come will destroy the city and the sanctuary. The end will come like a flood: War will continue until the end, and desolations have been decreed. 27He will confirm a covenant with many for one 'seven.' In the middle of the 'seven' he will put an end to sacrifice and offering. And on a wing of the temple he will set up an abomination that causes desolation, until the end that is decreed is poured out on him."

—Daniel 9:24-27

A particular interpretation of Daniel 9:24-27 is foundational to the whole program of the last days as taught by the school of Scofield.

The seventy units of seven are seventy times seven years, unless they are a symbolic number of fullness. In these "seventy sevens" God's goal for the redemption of Israel will be accomplished. That goal is stated in verse 24, in six short phrases, three of which refer to the removal of sin, and the other three that deal with the restoration of righteousness.

The first three phrases are "to finish transgression, to put an end to sin, and to atone for wickedness." The second three are "to bring in everlasting righteousness, to seal up vision and prophecy and to anoint the most holy." Everyone recognizes in these words what Jesus Christ did with sin on the cross and how he obtained the gift of righteousness for his people.

The very last phrase, "to anoint the most holy," is difficult. If it refers to a place, it may be

- the new people, as the temple,
- the new Jerusalem, or

about the end (Matt. 24; Mark 13; Luke 21) into these seven years. In fact, Jesus' words "Then shall be great tribulation such as was not since the beginning of the world" (Matt. 24:21, KJV) form the title of the seven years. During that

---

- the millennial temple—as the premils would have it.

If "the most holy" can stand for a person, it refers to God's Messiah.

The seventy sevens are subdivided into seven plus sixty-two plus one unit of seven (7+62+1=70). After the word that sends the exiles home, seven units of seven years (7x7) will elapse before temple and city will be rebuilt with a moat, though this will occur in troubled times. Sixty-two times seven (434 years) later, the "cutting off" of the Anointed One takes place. This, as everyone agrees, refers to the death of Christ on Golgotha. Then the "people of the ruler [or prince] who will come" (v. 26) will destroy the city. This appears to apply to the destruction of Jerusalem in A.D. 70 by Titus and his Roman legions.

The last unit of seven is named in verse 27. "He will confirm a covenant for many for one 'seven.'" It does not say who this "he" is. The dispensationalists take this to be the Roman ruler, but a different one from the one in verse 26 who destroyed the city. They say this "he" is the Antichrist who will come from Rome. He will make a covenant with "many," with the "believing Jews" (!) for a period of seven years. But "in the middle of the [seven-year period] he will put an end to sacrifice and offering" (v. 27). This means, they say, that the restored service in the rebuilt temple will be forbidden by the world dictator. This Antichrist will set himself up in Jerusalem's temple as God, "an abomination that causes desolation." He will begin the most ruthless persecution ever experienced anywhere. This will last for three and one-half years, after which Christ will come to establish the millennium.

However, here is the point, as ingenuous as it is unlikely: these last seven years of God's prophetic program are separated from the other 483 years (69x7=483) by the church age. There's a gap of at least nineteen centuries between verse 26 and verse 27. According to the dispensationalists, the seven years begin when God is through with the church and turns again to dealing with the people of Israel.

These, then, are the seven years, the time of the great tribulation. But true Christians will not be around. They will have been airlifted to heaven in the rapture, when the seven last years began. And when the seven disastrous years are over, Jesus will descend to the Mount of Olives and sit on David's throne in Jerusalem for the thousand years that dispensationalists refer to as the millennium.

"great tribulation" the Antichrist will reign. For the seven years, or half of seven years, according to others, people must bear the number 666, the mark of the beast, if they are to be tolerated in society. Revelation 6 through 19 are then read as a calendar of catastrophes and all of them must be fulfilled within these seven years.

If their interpretation of Daniel 9:27 is wrong, the whole dispensational prophetic program breaks down.

I am not going to argue with their interpretation of the seventy weeks. The verses are difficult, enigmatic, puzzling. And they have been worked over by a host of scholars.

Gabriel speaks to Daniel about seventy times seven years, just as Daniel was inquiring about the seventy years of exile in Babylon predicted by Jeremiah (25:11; 29:10).

But "seventy" as well as "seventy sevens" are round figures. The return from Babylon and the deportation to Babylon took place in waves. We Western calculators have a hard time finding the exact number of seventy years between one of the deportations and one of the returns. It's the same, I think, with the seventy "sevens" in Daniel 9. It gives us a rounded figure for the time God decreed between the return from Babylon and the completion of his work of redemption and judgment as set forth in verse 24. In verse 27 the one referred to as "he," who makes or confirms the covenant with many, is assumed to be the Antichrist who must come from Rome. But "he" could also refer to the Messiah, Jesus, who puts an end to the sacrifice and whose death causes the end of Jerusalem. The veil was rent as a sign that the temple had served its purpose.

Of course, the Messiah is not the one who would "set up an abomination that causes desolation." But the translation of that phrase is uncertain. The NRSV reads: "he shall make sacrifice and offerings cease; and in their place shall be an abomination that desolates, until the decreed end is poured out on the desolator." The Jerusalem Bible, the New English Bible, as well as versions in other languages, including the oldest version, the Septuagint, favor a Messianic interpretation of verse 27. According to these readings, it's *the Messiah* who puts an end to the sacrificial service and the former holy place becomes defiled and ruined.

The prophecy of the seventy "sevens" has in view the time period between the release from the exile in Babylon and the sacrificial death of the Messiah as well as the total destruction of temple and city. One either chooses for the Messianic interpretation of the text, or the end-time interpretation of Scofield and the like. But we should not make this text the cornerstone for a futuristic system.

Meanwhile, the Darby-Scofield school is completely confident about *The Seven Last Years*—the title of a 1978 novel by Carol Balizet, who places the first of the seven years in 1995. Next to the millennium, "the seven years of the great tribulation" is the most frequently used designation of time in dispensationalist prophetic programs. Don't forget, however, that "the seven years" have, at best, a wobbly basis in a single biblical text, one for which most translators and commentators offer a different interpretation.

Towards Armageddon

Israel must be back in Palestine before the last seven years can begin. That's why the formation of the state of Israel on May 14, 1948, set off so much Scriptural and political speculation among the dispensationalists. Almost without exception, the prophecy interpreters are convinced that this is the gathering of Israel that was predicted by the Old Testament prophets. The script for the seven years is as follows: The king of the South, of Egypt and black Africa, doesn't like the Jews being in their homeland and so he will attack Israel. While Israel and Africa are fighting, the King of the North, Gog, or Russia—a big and unwarranted assumption—will seize the opportunity to overrun the countries of the Middle East and occupy Egypt as well as Israel.

Meanwhile, the old Roman Empire will be restored as the ten-state federation in Western Europe under the leadership of the Antichrist, who will rule from Rome. He has a covenant with Israel. Under his protection, Israel has built a temple in Jerusalem and restored its religious observances. Now that Russia has invaded Israel, Rome must live up to its obligations. When Russia hears that the Roman dictator is preparing for war and that the Chinese are sending an army of 200 million people, Russia retreats from Egypt and sets up headquarters in the temple area on Mount Moriah.

Now the outpouring of God's wrath, described in Revelation 6-19, proceeds furiously. God's judgments fall on a rebellious world and an unfaithful nation of Israel. Russia and the whole Red Army is destroyed either by a direct act of God or a nuclear blast. The major cities of the world will also be bombed and the carnage is indescribable. But somehow the Western powers, including North America, which is supporting the Antichrist and his European forces, occupy Jerusalem. Then the rule of the Antichrist over the world is established. The beast rules from Jerusalem. Its power will be a religious ideology for which today's "ecumenical movement of the apostate churches" is preparing us—yes, most dispensational prophecy writings make a direct connection between the church unity promoted by ecumenical organizations and the rule of the Antichrist!

The world will be in the claws of the Antichrist, the beast, and of his false prophet. The dictator will be worshiped as god and "the harlot" described in the book of Revelation will be revealed. "The harlot" will be the religious system of drugs, astrology, and church unity, which we already see in preparatory stages today.

An apparent weakness in this scheme is that the Antichrist seems to have no Christians to persecute because they were "raptured" when the tribulation started. But now the conversion of Israel takes place. One hundred and forty-four thousand Jewish Christians make this the greatest evangelistic crusade the world has ever seen, despite the fact that the wrath of the beast will be turned on them.

Then comes Armageddon. The Chinese armies clash with the Europeans, who are reinforced by the North Americans. They meet in the strip of land north of Jerusalem, a valley that runs from the Mediterranean to the Jordan. It will be an unsurpassed bloodbath. The blood will be as deep as the horses' bridles over a distance of two hundred miles.

When it seems that no life will be left in the world, Jesus returns to Jerusalem. Instantly he wipes out the enemies of Israel. The last seven—or three and one-half years—of unparalleled suffering are over. With Jerusalem as his headquarters, Christ will reign for a thousand years over a faithful people and a land as good and peaceful as paradise. People will grow old but they will still die. And at the end of the thousand years, an insurrection will occur. Satan will be loosed for a little while. But the Lord will put that rebellion down. And then come the end of human history and the final judgment of God.

Not every preacher and writer in the North American evangelical prophecy schools agree on every detail. But this sketch sums up the gist of most of their predictions. We will discuss some crucial parts of the system in following chapters. The whole system hangs on a few unlikely conclusions drawn from one or two obscure Bible passages. Yet it is preached and taught by the dispensational Christians as if God revealed it to us. To get an overview of this scheme, see the following chart for timelines that contrast the Reformed understanding with that of the dispensational premillennialists.

Dispensationalist View

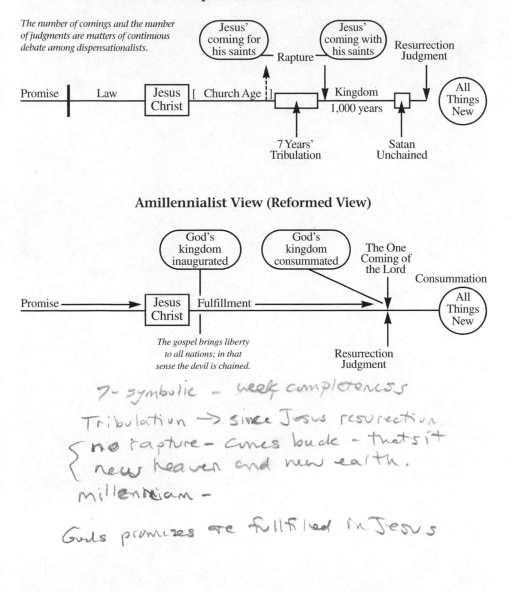

The number of comings and the number of judgments are matters of continuous debate among dispensationalists.

Jesus' coming for his saints

Rapture

Jesus' coming with his saints

Resurrection Judgment

Promise | Law | Jesus Christ | [Church Age] | Kingdom 1,000 years | All Things New

7 Years' Tribulation

Satan Unchained

Amillennialist View (Reformed View)

God's kingdom inaugurated

God's kingdom consummated

The One Coming of the Lord

Consummation

Promise → Jesus Christ | Fulfillment → | All Things New

The gospel brings liberty to all nations; in that sense the devil is chained.

Resurrection Judgment

7 - symbolic - week completeness

Tribulation → since Jesus resurection

{ no rapture - comes back - thats it
{ new heaven and new earth.

millennium -

Gods promises are fullfiled in Jesus

The Beast Comes Out of the Sea, from Apocalypse　　　　　—Giusto di Diovanni Menabuoi, 1363-1393

CHAPTER 5

"THE RAPTURE"

No group of Christians has a more detailed calendar of God's plans for the future than the premillennialists in the Darby-Scofield tradition. Yet they manage to teach that the Lord's coming is imminent and that the date is unpredictable. They do so by splitting the coming of Christ into two stages. They have a coming that can take place any time and a coming that can happen only after the Antichrist has come. First, Jesus will come for his saints. That's the rapture. Seven years later he will come with his saints, bringing in the millennium of peace.

According to these premillennialists, the rapture may happen at any time. Christians who died will rise from death and be glorified. Christians who are alive will be changed in a moment, in the twinkling of an eye. They will meet the Lord in the air. But those who aren't real Christians will not even notice the rapture. They will be left guessing what happened after the rapture has removed the Christians. They will have to live through seven years of earthshaking, humanity-mutilating events: the reign of the Antichrist and the great tribulation.

A Preacher's Heyday

The rapture, the quick removal of all Christians from the world, is a favorite topic of premillennial preachers:

> All over the earth the graves of those who have trusted Christ will explode as their occupants soar into the heavens to meet the Light of the World. . . . Cars will empty beside the interstate, their engines running, their drivers and occupants strangely missing. Supper dishes will steam in the homes of believers, food will boil on their stoves, but no one will remain to eat this earthly dinner, for all believers will be taking their places at the heavenly table for the marriage supper of the Lamb. The next day, headlines of local, national and international newspapers will scream, "MILLIONS MISSING WITH NO EXPLANATION." New Age devotees might explain the mass disappearance by insisting that a vast armada of UFOs have abducted millions of people. . . .
>
> Telephone lines around the world will jam as families try to check on loved ones. And the churches of the world will be packed with weeping, hysterical people who see the truth too late and cry, "The

Lord of Glory has come and we are left behind to go through the Tribulation and to face the coming Antichrist."

—John Hagee, Beginning of the End, p. 104-105

Hagee, in the above quotation, has at least one reference to the delights of the redeemed: missing their supper because of the rapture, they can sit at the heavenly table for the wedding feast. Most writings about the rapture say more about the catastrophe that will hit the earth than about the joy of the redeemed who are spared the chaos.

Numerous paintings, comic books, and novels depict the chaos resulting from the rapture. The picture of the nurse who runs to the doctor crying that all the babies are missing is almost as famous as the one of Jesus hovering over Dallas, Texas, while white figures rise from graves and Christian people fly to Jesus, as they leave behind the wrecks of their automobiles. "In one rapture painting, the lawnmower-pushing suburban husband gapes in wonder as his aproned wife soars over the clotheslines to meet Jesus." (Paul Boyer, *When Time Shall Be No More,* p. 256. Pictures of the paintings mentioned here can be found between pp. 144-145 and 280-281 of Boyer's book.)

Peter and Paul Lalonde produce a television broadcast called "This Week in Bible Prophecy." They have now prepared a video message, "Left Behind: Where'd Everybody Go?" The tape is intended to inform those who are left behind after the rapture. So-called "top experts in the field of Bible prophecy," namely Peter Lalonde, Hal Lindsey, John Walvoord, John Ankerberg, Zola Levitt, and Dave Breese, tell those who stayed behind to trust the Bible, believe in Jesus, distrust the Antichrist, and thus be saved. But the first fifteen minutes of the video are a dramatization of what the authors think will have happened at the time of the rapture one morning at 4:59, Eastern Standard Time, when millions of people literally vanish, including the speakers on the tape.

Cars and trucks are piled on top of each other; airplanes and helicopters crash and burn because Jesus took the drivers and pilots to himself. Worldwide accidents claim tens of thousands of victims. Fires burn out of control because stoves and welding torches are left unattended. An ever more frantic news anchorman reports that the U.S. *Explorer* has sighted one, possibly two, alien spacecraft, but even the President of the United States and the Secretary General of the United Nations are dumbfounded by this greatest disaster and attack in human history. While there's pandemonium and panic everywhere, a reporter from a city in Alabama announces—with a strong religious and regional bias, I thought—that the "major portion of the population of this city" seems to have disappeared. When asked for an explanation of these events, a bishop in Rome says that the disappearance of the old and backward part of humanity means a great leap forward for the evolution of a new humanity. And an Oxford professor, interviewed in London, agrees with the bishop that this is the next step in the social evolution bringing us closer to the deification of the human race.

The first segment of the video ends with the European Antichrist shouting to the masses that this is the death of the old God and the beginning of glory and power for humankind. The voice pledges to lead the world into the new age.

The rapture teaching that this video dramatizes is also called "the translation of the church." It makes for many dramatic and some hilarious stories. But some of us are bothered by those planeloads and busloads of passengers that are sacrificed when the Christian pilots go to heaven. It's hard to imagine Christ masterminding this cruel, cosmic joke.

Origin and Basis of the Rapture Doctrine

Those who believe in it present the rapture as if it were a fundamental Christian teaching, along with the Trinity and justification by faith. Actually the worldwide Christian church did not know, and still does not know, of a doctrine that teaches the rapture of the church before a great tribulation. But the Plymouth Brethren and J. N. Darby started to teach it around 1835.

Some have attempted to pinpoint the origin of the teaching. Iain Murray, in *The Puritan Hope,* claims that the idea that Christ would first rapture or remove the church before the "great tribulation" may have come from Edward Irving (1792-1834), as did many other features of Darby's teaching (p. 200). Dave MacPherson is more precise. In *The Unbelievable Pre-Trib Origin,* he shows that a Scottish woman, Margaret MacDonald, a follower of Irving and a charismatic enthusiast, had a revelation in which she learned that those who are in the light of Christ and have the fullness of the Spirit will be "caught up to meet him" (p. 106). "Darby borrowed from her, modified her views, and then popularized them under his own name without giving her credit" (p. 94). But John F. Walvoord is quick to point out that Margaret MacDonald did not say that this rapture would take place before the tribulation (*The Rapture Question,* p. 154).

Whatever its origin, the teaching of a first coming of Christ to take his church out of the world not only fits with the dispensational scheme, it is necessitated by the system. For God is supposed to finish his work with the church before he resumes his dealings with Israel. The seven years of tribulation are intended for the testing of Israel and for the revelation of God's wrath. But the church is saved from God's wrath. Therefore the church must be removed at the beginning of the seven year tribulation, according to the Darby-Scofield dispensational scheme. This system provides the spectacles through which the premillennialists read the Bible.

Dispensationalists have their own system of Bible interpretation, their own jargon, and their own concerns. Therefore it is virtually impossible for those of us who don't believe in a millennium and a rapture to participate in their conversations. John F. Walvoord, who wrote *The Rapture Question,* and Robert H. Gundry, who wrote *The Church and the Tribulation,* are considered top-notch evangelical scholars. In their books they argue about the question whether the church will go through the tribulation. Walvoord claims that no, the church will be raptured *before* the tribulation. That makes him a pre-tribulation rapturist. Gundry argues that yes, the church *will* be in the great tribulation. That makes him a post-tribulation rapturist. Yet both are premillennialists and both oppose teachings such as the partial rapture theory and mid-tribulationism.

Walvoord and Gundry think in categories we don't believe to be valid. To our mind they argue about matters that are unimportant to our faith. For example, they do not just argue about the number of comings of Christ and how many resurrections of dead people there are going to be, but they also seriously argue about the number of eschatological trumpets and the order in which they will be blown—and by whom (Gundry, pp. 148-151). As long as we do not scrutinize their presuppositions, the dispensational glasses themselves, we cannot meaningfully communicate with these premils. And as long as such teachers make these assumptions, their popularizers, people like Hal Lindsey and John Hagee, will place the teachings about the rapture and the tribulation on the same level as the Christian dogma of the Trinity (see John Hagee, *Beginning of the End,* p. 113).

There's some hope that "progressive dispensationalism," which is now being advocated by Craig A. Blaising, Darrell L. Block, and others, will eventually lead to a meaningful conversation for all who hope for the coming of the Lord. Also, Vern S. Poythress promotes a healthy Christian dialogue in his *Understanding Dispensationalists.*

The "Rapture" Text

The word *rapture* is derived from the Latin translation of a phrase in 1 Thessalonians 4:17: *rapiemur,* which means "we will be caught up," or "we will be snatched away." The passage in which this is found reads:

> [13]Brothers, we do not want you to be ignorant about those who fall asleep, or to grieve like the rest of men, who have no hope. [14]We believe that Jesus died and rose again and so we believe that God will bring with Jesus those who have fallen asleep in him. [15]According to the Lord's own word, we tell you that we who are still alive, who are left till the coming of the Lord, will certainly

not precede those who have fallen asleep. ¹⁶For the Lord himself will come down from heaven, with a loud command, with the voice of the archangel and with the trumpet call of God, and the dead in Christ will rise first. ¹⁷After that, we who are still alive and are left will be caught up together with them in the clouds to meet the Lord in the air. And so we will be with the Lord forever. ¹⁸Therefore encourage each other with these words.

—1 Thessalonians 4:13-18

The Christians addressed in this letter are young believers who have only recently "turned to God from idols to serve the living and true God, and to wait for his Son from heaven" (1:9-10). Living in this expectation, they became worried about fellow believers who died. Will Christians who die before the coming of the Lord miss out on this glorious event?

As their teacher, Paul does not want them to be "ignorant," and as their pastor Paul does not want them "to grieve like the rest of men, who have no hope" (v. 13). Therefore he clarifies what expectations Christians may have concerning Christ's return and our future with him. In verse 14 he tells them that as people who believe that Jesus died and rose again, we also believe that Christians who died are now alive. What happened to Christ happens to those who belong to him. Don't worry about them. They are with God, and when Jesus comes, God will bring them with him. How that will happen Paul explains in the following verses.

After appealing to their confession ("we believe") in verse 14, Paul presents a truth they did not yet confess. It is a "word of the Lord" (v. 15), not merely Paul's opinion. We don't know for sure how Paul knew this "word." Probably he received it by oral tradition, just like the saying of Jesus quoted in Acts 20:35, "It is more blessed to give than to receive."

He does not seem to quote the "word of the Lord" literally, but he draws a conclusion from what the Lord has said: "We who are still alive, who are left till the coming of the Lord, will certainly not precede those who have fallen asleep" (v. 15). No group of believers will have an advantage over another when the Lord returns. That's because the coming of the Lord will take place as follows: when Jesus himself descends from heaven, the dead in Christ will rise first, and the living will be "raptured," caught up together with the first group to meet the Lord in the air, and so we shall always be with the Lord (vv. 16-17).

This descent of the Lord and our meeting with him will be a supernatural event. It's not likely that we can give an exact description, in our words and with our sense of timing, of how it will all take place.

Bible students should also read Exodus 19:10-25. This passage describes the day when the LORD descended to the top of Mount Sinai after two days of fearful and scrupulous preparation on the part of his covenant people. "On the morning of the third day there was thunder and lightning, with a thick cloud over the mountain, and a very loud trumpet blast. Everyone in the camp trembled. Then Moses led the people out of the camp to meet with God . . . " (Ex. 19:16-17). It reads like a rehearsal for the great and final day described in 1 Thessalonians 4:16-17. It has the cloud, the noise, the terror, the trumpet, the descent of the Lord—and also the going forth to meet him.

Going Out to Meet the Lord

Dispensationalists say that Jesus does not descend all the way to the earth when he comes for his church. Rather, we who are raised and changed rise to meet him in the air. We go to heaven with him for seven years until the tribulation is over. But I think that the expression "to meet the Lord" is sufficiently explained by the Sinai experience in Exodus 19. There the people were led out of the camp by Moses to meet with God, who was descending. Moreover, the expression "to meet the Lord" was used in the Hellenistic world "for the official welcome of a newly arrived dignitary" (see Moulton & Milligan, *The Vocabulary of the Greek Testament, apantesis).* The use of the expression in the New Testament is similar: "At midnight the cry rang out: 'Here's the bridegroom! Come out to meet him!'" (Matt. 25:6). In Acts 28:15, when Paul's long journey to Rome is almost finished, the Christians in Rome "traveled as far as the Forum of Appius and the Three Taverns to meet us." The *meeting* is a welcome. It does not mean that the arriving persons, the bridegroom, Paul, or the Lord coming from heaven then turn around and go back again!

It is at the *parousia,* the coming of Christ, that the dead in Christ will be raised and the living who belong to Christ will be "raptured"—if we want to use that word. Together we will go out to meet the Lord. We "will be caught up together with them" (v. 17). Paul emphasizes the togetherness in answer to the original concern of the Thessalonians: "[we] will certainly not precede those who have fallen asleep" (v. 15). When we meet the Lord in the air, the church of all ages will be reunited. "And so we will be with the Lord forever" (v. 17). The main point of verse 17 "is not that we shall meet the Lord in the air, but that all believers together shall meet the Lord, never to be separated from him" (William Hendriksen, *I and II Thessalonians,* p. 119).

The One Coming of the Lord

The New Testament promises one undivided, glorious coming of the Lord. It is a coming *for* his saints, because those who are alive at his coming will meet him and be changed to live with him (1 Thess. 4:17; also 1 Cor. 15:52 where, at the sound of the trumpet, the Christians who are alive when the Lord returns are instantly changed to immortality). But it is also a coming *with* his saints (1 Thess. 3:13), because those who fall asleep in Jesus before he returns will be at his side on the day of his coming (1 Thess. 4:14).

All efforts to split Christ's coming into two stages appear to be motivated by a dispensational system that is imported into the text. No biblical text teaches a rapture or translation of the church prior to the coming of the Lord.

Worth Arguing?

Does it matter if Christians expect a pretribulation rapture of the church or a second coming of the Lord? Does it make any real difference for everyday Christian living whether we teach that we are going or that Christ is coming? I've thought much about this question and have come to the conclusion that there are three major objections to this teaching about the rapture, or "translation," of the church.

First, it is not only an error but also a sin to impose a system of interpretation (dispensationalist or any other) upon the Bible. All Christians know it, and all of us attempt to avoid it. The rapture of the church prior to the great tribulation is not found in the Bible. It is necessitated by the system that claims that God has one program for the church and another program for Israel. Only when the church has been "translated" can God return to his program with Israel. This doctrine of the rapture dates from the 1830s.

A second objection I have to this teaching of a rapture prior to the (real) return of the Lord is that it makes evangelical Christians teach a doctrine of second chances. At the present time they are preparing pamphlets, books, and videotapes for the conversion of those who are left behind when the saints are raptured. Unbelievers have their second chance during a period of seven years when the Jewish remnant will be evangelizing the world. Then the Lord will come to reign in Jerusalem, they claim.

During the millennium, however, unbelievers have a third chance to be converted. But all of this is fantasy. The time to turn to God is now, between his one and only coming in grace and his one and only coming in glory. Christ does not only come to take his servants home, but when "the Lord Jesus is revealed from heaven in blazing fire with his powerful angels . . . he will punish those who do not know God and do not obey the gospel of our Lord Jesus" (2 Thess. 1:7-8). The return of Christ will close the mission of the church and terminate the day of grace, the opportunity for all to turn to God and live. This is the unanimous teaching of the books of the New Testament. There are no second or third chances.

The third, and perhaps the most objectionable feature of the rapture teaching, is the world flight by the church. When the real trouble begins (the great tribulation) the true Christians sail through the sky to the wedding banquet in heaven. With thinly veiled glee evangelical preachers and authors keep making up stories about the mess the saints leave behind when they fly to the Lord.

There is not even a hint in the Scriptures that the saints will silently slip out of this world. The apocalyptic noises that the Bible associates with the appearance of the Lord are designed to sound the alarm for the cosmos and to awaken the dead (Matt. 24:31; 1 Cor. 15:52; 1 Thess. 4:16; Heb. 12:26). But the silent rapture teaching betrays an even more serious misunderstanding of the biblical connection between church and world. The biblical connection is one in which Christians are assigned the roles of salt and light—as we all know, and as some dispensationalists practice better than I do. We are in the world and not of it (John 17:15-16). But we must show a much greater solidarity with the pain and the hope of the present world than evangelical Christians are inclined to show.

When Paul, in Romans 8:18-27, considers our present suffering in the light of future glory, he includes church and creation in both suffering and hope. And he ties them closely together. Church and world share suffering and hope. Nobody lives or dies without these two qualities. In that respect, the church exists in solidarity with the whole cosmos. But the church is also the interpreter of suffering and hope. We tell the story of Good Friday and Easter, of cross and resurrection. These events changed us and the course of history. We speak of Christ. And within us the Spirit groans and prays so that God may open the way to the new world. There lies the liberty for this enslaved planet. For that reason creation longs to see the revelation of the children of God (v. 19).

The removal of the church in the rapture, prior to the great suffering of the planet, is an unbiblical, even anti-biblical, fantasy.

Hell (The Inferno)

—Artist unknown, Flemish school

CHAPTER 6

THE ANTICHRIST AND THE "GREAT TRIBULATION"

What are we to make of the claim of many prophecy pundits that Jesus cannot return as yet because the Antichrist has not yet come? Does the Bible support that view?

John writes, "Dear children, this is the last hour; and as you have heard that the antichrist is coming, even now many antichrists have come" (1 John 2:18). The name *Antichrist* is used only in 1 and 2 John. John uses the term to describe any and all who deny the basic Christian confession. "Who is the liar? It is the man who denies that Jesus is the Christ. Such a man is the antichrist—he denies the Father and the Son" (2:22). Anyone who denies the incarnation "is the deceiver and the antichrist" (2 John 7).

According to John the Antichrist is here. His presence proves that this is the last hour, the last days, the end time. So if we would ask the question, Shouldn't we see the Antichrist before we can expect the return of Jesus? John would say, "even now many antichrists have come" (1 John 2:18). In that respect there is no reason why Christ himself should not come at any time.

Although John is the only one who uses the word *Antichrist,* Christians seem to be accustomed to reserving the word for another figure, one who appears in 2 Thessalonians 2:3-10 as "the man of lawlessness" (or "the man of sin," KJV) and in Revelation 13 as "the beast." Both of these New Testament texts describe this anti-God figure in terms that were earlier used by Daniel.

In Daniel the Antichrist is not only a figure who is opposed to God, but he is a counter-God and a counter-Christ who wants to replace the real one. Daniel saw a little horn that "had eyes like the eyes of a man and a mouth that spoke boastfully" (7:8; see also vv. 20, 25). He also saw the same figure as a king who taunted the God of heaven by setting up "the abomination that causes desolation" (11:31; 12:11) in God's own temple. This desecration of the temple by an arrogant king took place in 168 B.C., when the Syrian king, Antiochus IV, set up a pagan altar in the holy place (1 Maccabees 1:54). This historical desecration was repeated in A.D. 70 by the Romans (Josephus, *War, IV,* 316), as the Lord had predicted (Matt. 24:15).

The anti-God Daniel describes is not only historical (the infamous Antiochus) but also eschatological. That is to say, he is the end-time figure that embodies the hate and the hubris of unredeemed humanity. He must make a final appearance as "Antichrist" before the end will come.

The two Antichrist figures of 2 Thessalonians 2:3-12 and Revelation 13 are woven from the threads pulled from the prophecies of Daniel. The two characteristic traits of the Antichrist are his arrogance over against God by blaspheming and taunting God, and his deception of people.

God-Defying Arrogance

We see this God-defying arrogance in the little horn with the big mouth (Dan. 7:20, 25) and again in the lawless one of 2 Thessalonians 2:4: "He will oppose and will exalt himself over everything that is called God . . . he sets himself up in God's temple, proclaiming himself to be God." Similarly, the beast from the sea utters *blasphemies* (Rev. 13:1, 5-6—the Greek word is used four times). The Antichrist is a radical atheist. He opposes and replaces God.

The beast in Revelation 13, a combination of Daniel's four beasts representing Rome and its emperor, is a totalitarian state. It lifts itself up to heaven. Therefore it's also called Babylon (Rev. 17:5; possibly also 1 Pet. 5:13), the city that is the exact opposite of the new Jerusalem, which comes down from heaven.

A Liar

This Antichrist is enormously powerful and manages to deceive masses of people. In Revelation 13 he does it with the help of another beast, one that rises out of the earth. This beast is better-looking than the first one. He even resembles the Lamb, though he speaks like the dragon (Rev. 13:11). This is the religious and cultural power that supports the first beast, because every tyrant needs a prophet. The prophet makes the slogans and composes the hymns of the beastly kingdom.

Note that the kingdom of the beast is an exact caricature of the kingdom of God. It has a Messiah, and it has signs and wonders. It aims at a new order that involves all of life. It even has a sort of baptism, a sign to show that one belongs to the group. It's a mark not of God, but of the beast: "No one could buy or sell unless he had the mark, which is the name of the beast or the number of his name" (Rev. 13:17).

The Antichrist is not the devil but the devil's tool. And just as the devil may be called "a liar and the father of lies" (John 8:44), this son of the devil is the great deceiver. "The coming of the lawless one will be in accordance with the work of Satan" (2 Thess. 2:9). He will do "counterfeit miracles" or "lying wonders" (v. 9). Those are not fake healings, but miracles that convince people to accept the lie he is telling. He will do "every sort of evil that deceives those who are perishing" (2 Thess. 2:10). Also in Revelation 13:14 it is said of the second beast that he "deceived the inhabitants of the earth." Deception is the devil's daily, natural activity. The Antichrist is the end-time revelation of the devil's power to deceive human beings.

But God remains sovereign Lord of all. People who are deceived are personally guilty: "They perish because they refused to love the truth and so be saved" (2 Thess. 2:10). Yet it is God who delivers them to their self-chosen punishment: "God sends them a powerful delusion so that they will believe the lie" (2 Thess. 2:11).

Within Limits

God also limits the time and the activity of the devil. The devil himself, the dragon named in many ways in Revelation 12:9, "knows that his time is short" (12:12). His biggest product, the Antichrist, gets only forty-two months (three and one-half years), 1,260 days, three and one-half days, or time, times, and half a time—all of which add up to half of seven (Rev. 11:2-3; 12:6, 14; see also Dan. 12:7). Since seven is the number of fullness and completion, three and one-half says that a life or a work is interrupted halfway. God permits the activity of his opponent but he also sets the limit. The terror will not last long. In 2 Thessalonians the appearance of the wicked one and his destruction are mentioned in one breath. And in Revelation the time of the beast and the days of our suffering will be shortened.

In that same sense of a great yet limiting concept, we should probably understand the "number of the beast, for it is man's number. His number is 666" (Rev. 13:18). Three times 6 is the apex of human development outside of God (who is 3+4=7). Therefore, in spite of its might and meanness, the beast is limited in attainment and endurance. Beyond this, however, there are dozens of different explanations of the number 666. As H. Berkhof has said, all of these explanations may be possible, few are probable, none are satisfactory (*Christ, the Meaning of History,* p. 112).

Discerning the Antichrist

In Daniel the anti-God figure is a historical person, Antioch Epiphanes, and he is a sign of the end. In Revelation the beast and the world empire it represents is modeled on the Roman Empire, with its deified emperor known to the writer and the earliest readers. But the kingdom of the beast was not fully realized in the totalitarianism of Rome. Just as the seven letters to the churches and the seven seals, trumpets, and bowls refer to happenings in John's day, while still having more to say about the church and the world, so the beast refers not only to Rome but also beyond it, as a sign of the end.

In 2 Thessalonians, Paul warns the young church that first this man of lawlessness must be revealed before Christ will come. In John's letters the

Since the earliest days of the church, Christians have identified the Antichrist with a historical person who opposed Christ and persecuted Christians there and then. But when the persecutions stopped and, for instance, the Roman Emperor Constantine himself became a convert to Christianity in A.D. 312, the expectation of the end weakened. The Reformers, though, had no doubt that the pope and/or the papacy was the Antichrist (see Calvin's *Institutes*, IV, ii, 12 and vii, 25).

Today this remains one of the most painful memories for Roman Catholic and Protestant churches that seek a closer relationship. But for our mothers and fathers the papacy was the power that persecuted those who wanted to obey the gospel. While Romanists saw their pope as the representative of Christ, Protestants saw him as a counter-Christ, one "who sets himself up in God's temple, proclaiming himself to be God" (2 Thess. 2:4—see Calvin's commentary on that text).

The Seventh-Day Adventists believe that the pope is the beast and that Sunday observance is the mark of the beast. They claim that it was the pope who decreed that Christians should keep Sunday as the Christian Sabbath. Today Seventh-Day Adventists say it more carefully: keeping Sunday instead of Sabbath is the mark of the beast "when Sunday observance is commanded by the law of the land" (Marvin Moore, *The Antichrist and the New World Order*, p. 91).

In our times, talk about the Antichrist begins with a survey of conditions that make the appearance of a world system possible. These conditions range from computer power, plastic cards, and microchips, to an increased tendency of using one language. Others are movements towards one church and one religion, as well as the revival of witchcraft. The speaker or author will argue that these conditions were all predicted by the prophets, and they have now set the scene for the appearance of the Antichrist. Then follows the description of the Antichrist himself. In some cases a theological interpretation is given, other times the Antichrist is depicted in the form of futuristic novels by writers such Carol Balizet, Dan Betzer, and Salem Kirban, among others. Especially the number 666 and the way this number will mark all who belong to the Antichrist fascinate the North American public. This kind of futuristic fiction is as popular as astrology and the occult sciences, which the prophecy line is supposed to expose and correct. For a thorough review of all the post-World War II dispensational expectations and speculations, see the second part of Paul Boyer's book, *When Time Shall Be No More: Prophecy Belief in Modern American Culture*, pp. 115-290.

Antichrist has appeared as a sure sign that this is the last hour. This biblical teaching about the Antichrist as the manifestation of God's end-time enemy is consistent but not systematic. The purpose of the teaching is a call for "endurance on the part of the saints who obey God's commandments and remain faithful to Jesus" (Rev. 14:12). The church of Christ must identify anti-Christian powers and persons throughout her history. Yet the focus of our expectation remains the coming of God in Christ.

"All forms of futurism are excluded," says G. C. Berkouwer (*The Return of Christ,* p. 281). He means that one may not teach or write about a future Antichrist.

North American dispensationalists, however, regard the Antichrist as a future figure who will show up just as we are departed in the rapture. He "will be a man who makes his debut upon the stage of world history with hypnotic charm and charisma. He will probably come from the European Union or a country . . . that was once part of the Roman empire" (John Hagee, *Beginning of the End,* p. 117). With many others, Hal Lindsey believes that "the Bible gives a perfect biographical sketch of this future world leader" (*The Late Great Planet Earth,* p. 103).

The futurists must deal with the identifications of the Antichrist that have been made by God's children throughout church history. We may ask, Why were all of them wrong and how do you know that you are right? Either they dismiss the history of such identifications as mistaken or they claim that the long line from Nero to the pope to Hitler to Stalin are only forerunners of the real devil incarnate, who is the true subject of their books. Berkouwer would say that we ought to desist from speculation about the future and that, biblically speaking, it is more correct to name the Antichrist in one's own time and history than to relegate him to the future (*Return of Christ,* p. 282).

The question remains whether, on the basis of the Bible, we should expect the revelation of a particular evil person before the revelation of Christ himself. Those who respond with a yes to this question build their case on 2 Thessalonians 2:3-10. Here Paul distinguishes clearly between the power of lawlessness that is already at work and the man of lawlessness who is not yet revealed. Why is he not yet manifested? Because there is a power or person that now holds him back. And the Thessalonians know who, or what, the "restrainer" is. Verse 6 can be translated either as "you know what is now restraining him," or as "now you know what is restraining him."

Once that "restrainer" is "removed" or "taken out of the way," the lawless one, whom the Lord Jesus will destroy with the breath of his mouth, will be revealed (vv. 7-8). Practically all careful interpreters admit that they don't

In his classic work *Pauline Eschatology*, Geerhardus Vos (1862-1949) devoted a whole chapter to "The Man of Sin." He concluded that "2 Thessalonians belongs among the many prophecies, whose best and final exegete will be the eschatological fulfillment . . . " (p. 133). In other words, we will know what it means when it has happened. After exhaustive study of 2 Thessalonians 2:5-7, Vos admits, *"non liquet,"* "it is not clear to me" (p. 133).

Many commentators say that the restrainer is a reference to "the principle of law and government" (Leon Morris), or "the power of well-ordered human rule" (William Hendriksen), but they admit that "certainty on this point is not available" (Hendriksen), and "the plain fact is that we do not know" (Morris).

know who or what it is that keeps the man of lawlessness from showing his real face. Yet the earliest readers of this letter knew about whom Paul was writing.

The early church fathers said that Paul spoke of Nero, who did not reveal his depravity until Seneca, his wise tutor, was removed from the scene. We don't know enough to say that they were wrong. The dispensationalists teach that the restrainer is the Holy Spirit, who will leave this earth when the church goes to heaven. However, interpreters have always pointed out that Paul's use of the words "until he is taken out of the way" would be quite inappropriate if the restrainer were the Holy Spirit—or the gospel, or the apostles, as others have contended.

Recognizing Anti-Christian Powers and Persons

The Antichrist is the end-time manifestation of the enemy of God. The enemy himself is behind the scenes, of course. Usually he works under the cover of darkness. He sowed the weeds that are now growing among the wheat (Matt. 13:24-30). But sometimes the enemy of God is manifested in the body of a person. Then one can point a finger at him and say, There is the "son of perdition" or "the one doomed to destruction," as Scripture calls both traitor Judas (John 17:12) and "the man of lawlessness" (2 Thess. 2:3). The open rebellion against Christ, "the sin against the Holy Spirit," is an anti-Christian manifestation. People who "have tasted the goodness of the word of God and the powers of the coming age" (Heb. 6:5) and who then openly deny that Christ is the Son of God, born of a woman—these people are Antichrists. And their theology is anti-Christian. "They went out from us, but they did not really belong to us" (1 John 2:19). Also in 2 Thessalonians 2:3 Paul says that first "rebellion," "falling away," or "apostasy" must come. The Antichrist does not come from a pagan nation but from a nation where Christianity was known, or from a church where Christ used to be honored. Or he reveals himself as a person who was once enlightened.

Also the totalitarian state is anti-God. It replaces God, who alone is absolute Sovereign. Christians are deeply suspicious of a totalitarian state. Tyrants arrogate Godlike powers that make them forget their proper place before the Sovereign Lord. Government under God is good, states Romans 13. Government that takes the place of God becomes a beast, warns Revelation 13.

The question of whether the Antichrist is a person or a power, a group, a movement, or whatever, is probably not a question that fits the biblical way of thinking. In the Bible a person embodies a group, and a group is personified in a figure. Christ is the representative of his own, he is the head of the body. But he also *is* the body. In a similar way, the Antichrist seems to be all of those at the same time.

It is possible that we will yet see a human being who resembles Nero and Stalin, a tyrannical tool of the devil. It is possible that we will yet see evil personified. But it is also possible that we won't. Christ may come in a time when people have reason to say that we experience "peace and security" (1 Thess. 5:3).

It is certainly not feasible to write the Antichrist's profile, and it is not permissible to write a timetable for his future manifestation. The point of the Scripture's warnings is that we should remain alert. That includes an acute discernment of the deception of our age—the false prophets, the false promises, and the false hopes by which people live and die. And we must note and name the secularism, the human pride, the replacement of God. These two traits, the deception of people and the arrogance before God, are the sure signs of the Antichrist.

The Tribulation of the Last Days

Those who expect a real, personal Antichrist just before Christ returns—a beast who will demand the worship that belongs only to God—also expect a great tribulation that will be more severe than any other persecution.

The dispensationalists expect it. But most of them, particularly the pretribs, think that true Christians will not go through it. According to them, during the seven years of this terrible time God's wrath will be poured out on the world and God will chasten Israel. Christians will be raptured before all hell breaks loose. Numerous other Christians, premils as well as amils (those who don't believe in a millennium at all), believe that all things will come to a climax just before Christ returns, including the persecution and tribulation of Christians.

Reformed and mainline theologians have not been as precise and detailed as the premils about what will happen at the end of the last days, but they have generally adhered to the expectation that all things must get worse before they can get better. See, for instance, this long sentence of Herman Bavinck: "Scripture clearly teaches that the power of Antichrist has its own history, manifests itself at different times and in different ways, and finally evolves in a general apostasy [falling away from the faith] and the breakdown of all natural and moral ties that now still hold back such apostasy, and then embodies itself in a world empire that utilizes the false church and apotheosizes [exalts] itself by deifying the head of that empire" (*The Last Things,* p. 114).

I do not contest this expectation of the final suffering and the climactic revelation of the Antichrist. I do think, however, that we ought to be prepared for a different development.

Unparalleled Suffering?

The great tribulation is named after the saying of Jesus in Matthew 24:21 in the King James Version: "For then shall be great tribulation such as was not since the beginning of the world to this time, no, nor ever shall be." In the NIV "great tribulation" is rendered "great distress"; NRSV has "great suffering."

For our pretrib, premil, dispensationalist fellow Christians, this great tribulation is a technical term for a seven-year period that follows the "translation of the church." They believe that numerous sections of the Old Testament prophecies predict events that must take place in this seven-year period (see, for example, J. Dwight Pentecost, *Thy Kingdom Come,* p. 329-331, where he lists over a hundred Old Testament texts that refer to the tribulation). These followers of Darby-Scofield theology read all of Revelation 6-19 as a catalogue of events to take place during the great tribulation and within seven years (see the footnotes in the *New Scofield Study Bible* under Rev. 4:1 and 7:14). This would mean that the book of Revelation had no message for its original readers. As a matter of fact, the book would have little to say to anybody until Darby discovered the program now popularized by Hal Lindsey.

I think that this whole scheme of the seven-year tribulation is not based on the Scriptures but is read into them.

Suffering, or tribulation, is part of the Christian life. It is not incidental, but belongs to the way of salvation. Jesus warns that "we must go through many hardships to enter the kingdom of God" (Acts 14:22). "Hardships" is the translation of the Greek word *thlipseis,* which is the same word that is used in Matthew 24:21 for the "great tribulation" (Greek: *megale thlipsis*). In 1 Peter 4:12 we read, "Do not be surprised at the painful trial you are suffering, as though something strange were happening to you." We have much more reason to believe that something strange is going on when the church has peace than when it is under fire.

It is still possible, however, that in Matthew 24:21 Christ was predicting a suffering for his followers that would be worse than all other tribulations. He said that the distress would be "unequaled from the beginning of the world until now—and never to be equaled again."

In this passage, was Jesus using what we call hyperbole, an excessively strong statement that is common in Jewish literature? When the firstborn were killed, there was "loud wailing throughout Egypt—worse than there has ever been or ever will be again" (Ex. 11:6). Of Hezekiah's piety it has been written, "There was no one like him among all the kings of Judah, either before him or after him" (2 Kings 18:5). But this statement should not be taken in a strictly literal sense, for in the same book we are told, "Neither before nor after Josiah was there a king like him who turned to the LORD as he did" (23:25).

For examples like these, see Gary DeMar, *Last Days Madness, the Folly of Trying to Predict When Christ Will Return,* pp. 74-75. However, DeMar concludes that all the predictions in Matthew 24 have been fulfilled with the destruction of Jerusalem, something I wouldn't dare say.

There have been times in the history of the Christian church and of the Jewish nation when sorrows were so deep and suffering so intense that, by any standard, things could not possibly get worse. Just read the book of Lamentations, the books of the Maccabees, or the books of Holocaust survivor Elie Wiesel to get a sense of what the Jews have suffered. Or read Fox's *Book of Martyrs* to get an idea of what the Christian church has suffered. There have been, and still are, fierce persecutions of Christians in the closing decade of the twentieth century. For a well-documented account see Paul Marshall, *Their Blood Cries Out.*

Yet, it is possible that a time might come when persecution is worldwide and pain even more pervasive. We cannot say that it *won't* happen. Neither should we say that it *must* take place.

A Final Revelation of the Antichrist?

What the Bible teaches about the Antichrist must be understood within the whole framework of the expectation of the Lord. The expectation of Christ is our central hope. We must be alert to Antichrists and anti-Christian manifestations. But we may never allow Antichrist studies, predictions, or speculations to become the preoccupation of the church.

The New Testament has the overall message that Christ will come unexpectedly and without warning—just as a thief does not give notice before breaking and entering. We err when we use the coming of the Antichrist, however we imagine that person and event, as a reason to say that Christ's coming cannot happen yet. While the proclamation of the gospel is indeed one knowable reason why history is prolonged by God, nobody can determine when it is enough so that the end will come. Paul thought the gospel was already bearing fruit "all over the world" (Col. 1:6).

It is not impossible that we or a later generation will witness the emergence of the wicked one who is more wicked than the lawless Antichrists that have stained and bloodied the pages of human history. We cannot say that it won't happen but we should not be surprised if it doesn't.

Now that we have examined dispensationalist claims about the rapture, the Antichrist, and the great tribulation, we will move on in chapter 7 to take a closer look at their teachings on the millennium, a thousand-year reign of Christ on earth.

The Last Judgment

—Jean Cousin, 1522-1594

THE THOUSAND YEARS

Millennium is a Latin word meaning *a thousand years.* Belief in a thousand years of peace and plenty is called *millennialism*—an unavoidable topic, especially in North America. In Europe it's called *chiliasm,* a Greek word that means *a thousand.*

Millennial Classifications

Whether we like it or not—and I don't—in North America every Christian is classified with a millennial label. This Latin label tells insiders whether you expect the coming of our Lord *before* the millennium (*pre*millennialism), *after* the millennium (*post*millennialism), or if you don't believe in a millennium at all (*a*millennialism). So I am stuck with an *amillennialist* label. I protest that label, just as others have done before me (Jay E. Adams, *The Time Is at Hand,* pp. 7-11; Anthony A. Hoekema, *The Bible and the Future,* p. 173).

I *do* believe in a millennium as taught in Revelation 20. But to the person who pastes *amillennialist* on my chest and on my writing, I want to say that this whole classification system shows what's wrong with our North American way of thinking about the last things, about eschatology. We are waiting for the Lord Jesus to appear and to transform this world and ourselves. We long for creation to be free at last and for our lowly bodies to be like his glorious body. And while we are trying to persevere in this expectation, we label each other in terms of our understanding of six verses in the twentieth chapter of the Apocalypse, which are clear to none of us.

With D. H. Kromminga I'll admit that Reformed theology "can be called amillennarian in a negative sense; in the sense that we do not quite know and never have quite known what to think of it all" (*The Millennium in the Church,* p. 303).

Both postmillennialists and premillennialists believe that we should expect an earthly millennium. Postmillennialists believe that Christ will come after that period. Premillennialists expect Jesus to come before the one thousand years of peace and plenty. Actually, as we have seen, dispensational premils believe in three comings of Jesus. First he comes "for his saints," as they say, at the beginning of the great tribulation. That's the rapture. Then he comes "with his saints" to take up residence in Jerusalem for the duration of the millennium. And when that age has drawn to a close he comes for the final judgment.

Postmils believe that Christ will conquer the world by means of the gospel. And when the world is Christianized, we will witness an unequalled time of harmony and happiness—the millennium. At the close of this millennial era there will be a time of apostasy and a final attack on Christians, because Satan must be allowed to deceive the nations for a little while. Then Christ will come and the final judgment will take place.

In chapter 4 I've sketched the dispensational premil expectation. Its most characteristic feature is the dispensational contrast between the Christian church and the Jewish nation. The Christian church will be removed in the rapture. Then follows the seven-year tribulation for the Jews, when God's wrath will be poured out on the world. The millennium will be a Jewish theocracy with the Son of David on the throne in Jerusalem. The church saints will assist King Jesus in his worldwide government during these thousand years.

Subtypes

Premillennialists are of two kinds. We've discussed dispensational premils. The other kind of premils call their system *historical* or *classical* premillennialism, suggesting that they continue the tradition of Justin Martyr and Irenaeus of the second century (see Appendix, p. 94). They don't believe that the church of Christ will be spared the tribulation and persecution of the end times. If there is going to be a rapture at all, they place it after the tribulation. So, in the millennial jargon, they are premillennial, post-tribulational rapturists.

Historic premillennialism also teaches that the New Testament knows of only one undivided people of God, made up of Gentiles and Jews. They differ from their premil cousins, who want to keep Israel forever separate from the church. But with the dispensational premillennialists, they hold on to two resurrections in Revelation 20.

In summary,

- *premils* believe that Jesus will come before the millennium. The Darby-Scofield premils believe that the first thing that is now on God's program is the removal of the true church by means of the rapture. Then follow the seven years of terror, mainly for Israel. After that, the Lord will come to Jerusalem and the remnant of Israel will be converted. In Jerusalem the Lord will reign for a thousand years. Historical premils also say that the Lord will come to Jerusalem at the beginning of the millennium, but the church must go through the tribulation. For them the whole millennial period is more churchly and less Jewish than for the dispensationalists.

- *postmils* believe that the gospel of Christ will be victorious. The world will turn to Christ and we will experience a thousand years of peace and plenty, after which Jesus will come to judge the living and the dead.

- *amils* believe that there is no biblical basis for these various constructions.

The notion of a golden age that brings heavenly peace in an earthly setting is not confined to Jewish and Christian circles. The human race
has always hoped for a long time of goodness, peace, and prosperity. The
dream is in the minds of the good and the evil. The Soviet revolution was
a bloodbath, but the excuse for the horror was a promised age of freedom
and equity that would surely follow and last a thousand years. Even Hitler,
that demonic man, claimed that his "Third Reich" would last a thousand
years. Hitler was a millennialist.

The millennial dream was, and is, particularly vivid in North America.
From its colonial beginnings, America functioned as a shelter for religious
groups that were outcasts in Europe. The New England Puritans, no less
than the Quakers and Baptists, considered themselves God's peculiar people who had a part to play in the coming of God's kingdom. In the new
world, their ideals would be realized. Politicians and preachers united in
praising the providence of God, which had kept North America a secret
until the right moment in history, the time when these preachers and
politicians came on the scene.

The Church of Jesus Christ of Latter-Day Saints (the Mormons) was driven
from the start by a millennarian teaching: it is the task of the saints to prepare
the way for Christ's second coming. Somewhere in the Western part of this
huge continent, the saints had to build a holy city, called Zion, the precursor
to the New Jerusalem. There the millennium would be experienced.

Countless people in the United States believe that this land of hope and
glory was especially prepared by God as the best place on earth. Just look at the
seal of the United States on the back of a dollar bill. *Annuit Coeptis,* it says: "He
[God] has favored our beginnings." It continues, *Novus Ordo Seclorum,* "a new
order of the ages." A new era has begun! These words surround the triangle, or
pyramid, which has God's all-seeing eye over it. It suggests a divine Builder
who started this project in the year MDCCLXXVI, A.D. 1776.

And isn't there a hint of millennialism in Canada's coat of arms, which
includes the words *A Mari Usque Ad Mare,* "From Sea to Sea"? The words are
from Psalm 72:8: "He shall have dominion also from sea to sea" (KJV). Because
of that quotation, we speak of "the *Dominion* of Canada." The coat of arms
bears witness to the hope that the Son of David's rule of righteousness and
peace will be established in Canada from sea to sea.

All these vastly diverse groups share a vision of the millennium as a time
of heavenly peace in an earthly setting, a transition stage between here and
eternity.

The Truth and Beauty of Millennialism

We find the expectation of a millennial reign of Christ in the ancient church, around A.D. 150, although no councils ever made creedal statements for or against millennialism. The greatest enemy of early Christianity was gnosticism. This teaching puts no stock in ordinary faith but encourages inquiry into spiritual truth on a higher, nonmaterial plane. The only way in which a person will ever get wise—the word *gnostic* means "one who knows"—is by freeing oneself from what is material and literal and by perceiving what is invisible and spiritual. In Bible reading one must look for a deeper, spiritual meaning behind every word and event.

Over against these heretics the defenders of the Christian faith insisted that God created a material universe and that God's promises about a restored creation and a rebuilt Jerusalem should be taken literally. Over against those who despised the flesh, the Christian apologists defended the resurrection of the body. Over against the timeless and immaterial fancies of the gnostics, these Christians stuck to faith in a God who acts in history and who promises us a tangible future.

This trait of millennial thinking is valuable and must be maintained. Every religion attempts to build a bridge between time and eternity, the *here* and the *beyond*. Greek religion did so, and Asian religions in American pop form do that too. And one may not say that this type of religious thinking is entirely absent in the Bible. But characteristic contrasts found in the Bible are not between *the here* and *the beyond*, but between *then* and *now* and *soon*. The Christian perspective is determined by God's acts in history and God's timeline: what God *did*, what God *is doing*, and what God *is going to do*. The Christian faith is rooted in historical events. The great contribution of millennialism is that it has stressed this earth as the terrain for the fulfillment of God's promises. With the millennialists, I too believe that we shall live on a renewed earth. When the world is renewed and when we have our resurrected bodies, we will fully enjoy God's creation and God himself.

Why a Millennium?

At least three arguments have been used in Jewish and Christian traditions for their expectation of a millennium. The first one, which may surprise you, is based on God's pattern of the creation week that culminated in the Sabbath day. Jewish rabbis used to say that the world would last for six thousand years, after which the Sabbath would be celebrated. Some thought this thousand-year Sabbath would prepare people for eternity. Others said it was eternity itself. In the Christian era the same arithmetic was used with the same ambiguity.

The epistle of Barnabas, one of the oldest Christian writings outside of the biblical canon, predicts that "in six thousand years the Lord shall bring all things to an end." The argument of the author of this letter is very simple: God created all things in six days and with the Lord a day is a thousand years (Ps. 90:4; 2 Pet. 3:8). Therefore, after six millennia of world history, the Sabbath will begin. "When his Son shall come and shall abolish the time of the Lawless One, and shall judge the ungodly, and shall change the sun and the moon and the stars, then shall he truly rest on the seventh day." For the writer of the epistle of Barnabas, the seventh millennium is the eternal Sabbath, the one referred to in Hebrews 4:9-11. He does not observe the Jewish Sabbath. The real anticipation of the eternal rest begins, he says, on the "eighth day which is the beginning of another world; wherefore we also keep the eighth day for rejoicing, in which also Jesus rose from the dead, and having been manifested ascended into heaven." The new Sabbath is most clearly anticipated on what we would call Sunday ("Epistle of Barnabas," section 15, from *The Apostolic Fathers,* J. B. Lightfoot and J. R. Harmer, p. 284).

We meet the argument that God created a world for six plus one times one-thousand years ([6+1]x1000) in many forms, from Barnabas, in the first century, to Johannes Cocceius, a Calvinistic professor of theology, in the middle of the seventeenth century. This ancient argument for a millennium of peace and prosperity will undoubtedly be revived when we pass from the second to the third millennium of the Christian era. But it is not based on any of God's promises or teachings. Besides, world history has already outlasted the six thousand years.

Support from Prophecy

A second support for belief in a coming millennium was found in the prophecies of the Old Testament. There too Christians accepted an idea that was first held by Judaism. Although the Old Testament, as I understand it, pictures the Messianic kingdom as the final and enduring kingdom of God, late Jewish writers saw it as a political kingdom of Israel, a glorious and blissful age that preceded the day of the LORD. Since the time of the early church, many Christians have also believed in this kind of a millennium.

Justin Martyr (c. 100-165) believed in a thousand-year reign of Christ on earth centered "in Jerusalem which will then be built, adorned and enlarged as the prophets Ezekiel and Isaiah and others declare" (*Dialogue with Trypho, a Jew,* ch. LXXX).

Up until today, millennarians believe that Old Testament prophecies about the restoration of Israel, the gathering of its people, and the glories of Jerusalem must be literally fulfilled in the millennium. For instance, Isaiah prophesied,

"For to us a child is born, to us a son is given, and the government will be upon his shoulders. . . . He will reign on David's throne and over his kingdom . . ." (Isa. 9:6-7). We have witnessed his birth, death, and resurrection when he came for the first time. But he will reign on the throne of David during the millennium. Israel will be in Palestine. "I will plant Israel in their own land, never again to be uprooted" (Amos 9:15). Even the temple, which Ezekiel saw (40:1-47:12), must be built and the offerings must be made "in keeping with God's prophetic program for the millennium" (*New Scofield Study Bible,* note on Ezek. 40:5). Then Jesus will rule over the world from Jerusalem and the prayer of Psalm 72 will be answered: "He will rule from sea to sea and from the River to the ends of the earth. . . . All kings will bow down to him" (vv. 8, 11). While he rules in righteousness, "the mountains will bring prosperity to the people, the hills the fruit of righteousness" (v. 3).

Premillennialists cling to these Old Testament prophecies. Since they don't find their literal fulfillment in the New Testament, they designate the millennium as the time in which God will make good on his promises.

I believe, and will later argue in detail, that prophetic language about Jerusalem's redemption and the return of Israel's glory is the only intelligible way in which prophets could speak to their contemporaries about God's great future. And further, I am convinced that the New Testament is the completion of the Old Covenant. It's the *New Testament revelation* that determines how we should understand what God said through the ancient prophets.

Revelation 20:1-10

The third reason why many Christians expect a thousand years of heavenly goodness in an earthly environment is their understanding of Revelation 20:1-10. This is the only place in the Scriptures where the thousand years are mentioned—six times, in seven verses. Notice that it says nothing about the Jewish nation in this passage, and it makes no mention of Jerusalem. According to this passage, the martyrs are alive and reign with Christ a thousand years, while Satan is bound and locked in the abyss, which refers to a deep hole with a lid on it.

Those who expect a literal thousand-year reign of Christ on earth use Revelation 20:1-10 for the time-frame and the prophecies of the Old Testament for the content. Because it's been used in centuries of millennial faith and fantasy as described in Appendix (p. 94), we should have a close look at this passage.

> ¹And I saw an angel coming down out of heaven, having the key to the Abyss and holding in his hand a great chain. ²He seized the dragon, that ancient serpent, who is the devil, or Satan, and bound him for a thousand years. ³He threw him into the Abyss, and locked

and sealed it over him, to keep him from deceiving the nations anymore until the thousand years were ended. After that, he must be set free for a short time.

⁴I saw thrones on which were seated those who had been given authority to judge. And I saw the souls of those who had been beheaded because of their testimony for Jesus and because of the word of God. They had not worshiped the beast or his image and had not received his mark on their foreheads or their hands. They came to life and reigned with Christ a thousand years.⁵ (The rest of the dead did not come to life until the thousand years were ended.) This is the first resurrection. ⁶Blessed and holy are those who have part in the first resurrection. The second death has no power over them, but they will be priests of God and of Christ and will reign with him for a thousand years.

⁷When the thousand years are over, Satan will be released from his prison ⁸and will go out to deceive the nations in the four corners of the earth—Gog and Magog—to gather them for battle. In number they are like the sand on the seashore. ⁹They marched across the breadth of the earth and surrounded the camp of God's people, the city he loves. But fire came down from heaven and devoured them. ¹⁰And the devil, who deceived them, was thrown into the lake of burning sulphur, where the beast and the false prophet had been thrown. They will be tormented day and night for ever and ever.

The Context of Revelation 20:1-10

This passage is the record of a vision: "And I saw . . ." (v. 1). All of Revelation consists of things John "saw" and "heard," things that we cannot ordinarily see or hear. He uses "I saw" and "I heard" more than thirty times each.

John was "in the Spirit" (1:10; 4:2; 17:3; 21:10). That means that he had an ecstatic experience. He was outside of himself. Paul was also "in the Spirit" once, caught up to paradise. He heard inexpressible things that he was not permitted to tell (2 Cor. 12:4). But John must make a record of the awesome things he sees and the terrible voices he hears.

The language of his record is pictorial and symbolic. It is not the ordinary language we use in discourse and narrative. We call it apocalyptic language, although that doesn't help us much. It's the sort of writing that deals with the end of the world and the wrath of God. The curtains that usually limit what we can see and hear are torn. The partitions between heaven and earth and the netherworld are temporarily removed. Angels are common (they're mentioned sixty-seven times in Revelation), but so are dragons and other such creatures.

Apocalyptic writing uses animals as symbols, but it also uses stars, numbers, and colors. And all of that multifaceted reality must be received and understood; that is, believed and kept by the people who are addressed in this book (1:3; 22:6-7).

The vision of the binding of Satan, beginning with "I saw" in 20:1, and the vision of the exaltation of the martyrs, beginning with another "I saw" in 20:4, follow the visions of the heavenly Warrior ("I saw," 19:11), and of the burning of the beast and the false prophet (19:17-21). Chapters 19 and 20 are logically connected because the visions illumine the destruction of God's enemies. But that does not mean, as premillennialists would have it, that Jesus returns to destroy the Antichrist (ch. 19) before he establishes the millennium (ch. 20). They attach an unwarranted chronology or calendar of events to these visions of John.

The Chaining of the Devil

The biblical picture of the universe has three stories: heaven is beyond the sky, the earth is the flat surface on which we dwell, and the cellar beneath is filled with all sorts of critters you would not want to meet. We live on earth in the hope that someday "at the name of Jesus every knee should bow" in all three stories of the universe, "in heaven and on earth and under the earth" (Phil. 2:10). Then the victory will be complete.

Now John sees an angel coming from heaven to earth with a key to open the shaft that leads to the netherworld and with a chain to tie up the dragon. The angel takes hold of the enemy who is properly identified by all its terrible names: "dragon," "ancient serpent," "devil," and "Satan" (v. 2). This archenemy of ours gets tied up and locked away for a thousand years "to keep him from deceiving the nations anymore until the thousand years were ended. After that, he must be set free for a short time" (v. 3).

Nobody takes this literally, of course, because the evil one cannot be handcuffed and there is no trapdoor to the underworld. There isn't even a three-story universe. But we must interpret what God is telling us through this apocalyptic picture.

The purpose of this binding is "to keep him from deceiving the nations anymore." The chaining does not mean that all demonic powers have disappeared from the earth, but the work of Christ and the proclamation of the gospel of the kingdom bring freedom to countless people and numerous nations who were deceived by the devil until that time. Satan lost the battle with Jesus. "The strong man," Satan, was tied up and robbed of the people he possessed (Matt. 12:29; see also Luke 10:18, "I saw Satan fall like lightning from heaven"; John 12:31, "now the prince of this world will be driven out"; among others). Other apocalyptic texts say that Satan was cast out of his position of power when Jesus ascended to heaven (Rev. 12:9) and that at least some fallen angels were banished to the pit ages ago, awaiting judgment "bound with everlasting chains" (2 Pet. 2:4; Jude 6).

This is one phase of the victory of Christ over Satan. In a book that swarms with symbolic numbers, we should be careful not to take "a thousand years" literally. For ten-times-ten-times-ten years, that is, for a very long time, Satan is incarcerated. Then, "for a *short* time," he must be untied.

The Reign of the Martyrs

Revelation has been written to encourage the church in the last days to be steadfast in persecution and to wait for the Lord. "To him who overcomes and does my will to the end, I will give authority over the nations—'he will rule them with an iron scepter; he will dash them to pieces like pottery—'" (2:26-27).

In 3:21 we read, "To him who overcomes, I will give the right to sit with me on my throne. . . . " It is a little hard to understand just what is involved in this rule from a throne and this reigning with Christ. But the idea that the saints of the Most High will reign with him (Dan. 7:27), and that the disciples who followed Jesus will judge with him (Matt. 19:28), and that the Christian congregation will judge the world and the angels (1 Cor. 6:1-6) is well established in Scripture.

In John's vision, the thrones are in heaven and the ones who have been faithful until death take their seats on them. They have the power to judge. And they reign with Christ for a thousand years (v. 4).

That last part of the verse, "They came to life and reigned with Christ a thousand years," is the most controversial sentence of the passage. I think it must refer to the martyrs who were loyal to Christ and were killed by the persecutors. In this world the martyrs seem to be the losers. The eagle of Rome seems to be the victor. But it isn't true, states the vision. "They came to life and reigned with Christ a thousand years." They cannot die because Jesus is their resurrection. "He who believes in me will live, even though he dies" (John 11:25).

"Reigning with Christ" (v. 4) refers to their position with Christ between their death and their final resurrection. Jesus himself said that Abraham, Isaac, and Jacob are alive with God, because "He is not the God of the dead, but of the living, for to him all are alive" (Luke 20:38). And this is the kind of life that's meant in Revelation 20:4, where it says "they came to life" or "they lived and reigned."

Verse 5 indicates that the "rest" who have died do not "live" until the coming of Christ and the general resurrection.

The beatitude of verse 6 is for all of us. The book of Revelation opens with a beatitude: "Blessed is the one who reads . . . blessed are those who hear it and take to heart what is written . . . " (1:3). It closes with another: "Blessed are those who wash their robes . . ." (22:14). Another beatitude that is for the reader is "Blessed are the dead who die in the Lord" (14:13). So is "Blessed and holy are those who have part in the first resurrection" (20:6). The "second resurrection," not specifically mentioned but implied, is the resurrection of the body. The first resurrection refers to our belonging to Christ, who is the resurrection and the life. Then the second death has no power over us. The second death is hell or "the lake of fire" (20:14; 21:8). "Blessed are those who die in the Lord" means the same as "Blessed are those who have part in the first resurrection." For a thousand years, that is to say, until the end of the age and the return of the Lord, "they will be priests of God and of Christ and will reign with him" (20:6). But those who die without having part in Christ have no life after the first death, and they have no escape from the second death when they are raised for judgment (20:12-13, 15).

The Interpreters' Divide

This interpretation reads the visions of Revelation 20 in the light of the rest of the New Testament. But there are many other interpreters who believe that in verse 4 God announces a special, physical resurrection of deceased believers (martyrs?), prior to the general resurrection of the dead. And if we protest that Revelation 20 is a vision, and that it is full of symbolic language and therefore should not be used as the basis for a new teaching, these interpreters proceed to read the rest of the New Testament in the light of Revelation 20. Having found a "first resurrection" in Revelation 20, they reread 1 Corinthians 15:22-24 and find room for a first and a second resurrection.

Usually premillennialists of the Darby-Scofield tradition end up with several resurrections for various groups of people (martyrs, Old Testament saints, and people who die during the millennium). Among themselves they argue about the exact number of resurrections and the sequence of their occurrence. The premil teaching of a first and second resurrection is derived from Revelation 20:4 and carried into several other Bible texts. The big difference between millennialists and Reformed and other Christian traditions is that the former attempt to read the rest of the New Testament in the light of what they believe is the teaching of Revelation 20, while the latter interpret Revelation 20 in the light of the rest of the New Testament.

In 1 Corinthians 15:22-24, Paul speaks of a certain order that God observes in his redemptive restoration: "For as in Adam all die, so in Christ all will be made alive. But each in his own turn: Christ, the firstfruits; then, when he comes those who belong to him. Then the end will come, when he hands over the kingdom to God the Father. . . ." The reasoning of those who have found two resurrections in Revelation 20 and seek confirmation in 1 Corinthians 15 is as follows. God raised Christ as the firstfruits; then, at Christ's coming he will raise his church (the rapture). Then the end will come, which is the second resurrection. Just as there is a lot of time between Christ's resurrection and that of the Christians, so there is an interim (the millennium) between the resurrection of the saints and the general resurrection at the end. However, Paul is not referring here to a *third* event. He addresses people who apparently believe in Christ's resurrection but do not expect a resurrection of Christians (see v. 12). Now he defends his teaching that "in Christ all will be made alive," speaking only of believers, of those who are in Christ. He states that, indeed, God observes a certain order: First Christ, then those who belong to him at Christ's return, and only then comes the end, the consummation. The notion that a third phase is coming after the resurrection "of those who belong to him" does not properly belong to Paul's reasoning.

Once we are convinced that a second and a third resurrection must take place, then we can read that teaching into 1 Corinthians 15 and, with a bit more difficulty, into many other passages as well. Harry Bultema, for instance, has eight "prooftexts for the first resurrection" from the Old Testament and eight "New Testament prooftexts for the first resurrection," not counting Revelation 20:4 (*Maranatha!* pp. 111-133).

The progressive dispensationalists have become much more careful: "Revelation 20 is the only Scripture which explicitly predicts an intermediate, millennial kingdom. . . . An intermediate kingdom may be implied from Paul's delineation of historical stages of resurrection in 1 Corinthians 15:20-28" (Craig A. Blaising and Darrell L. Bock, *Progressive Dispensationalism*, p. 273).

Insufficient Evidence

Millennial faith and fantasy are as old as Christianity itself—actually, as old as Judaism. The Reformed confessions have never condemned millennialism, while Lutherans and Roman Catholics did warn Christians not to indulge in such "Jewish dreams."

I believe there is insufficient Scriptural reason to expect an earthly millennium; I am convinced that some features of the millennium, which the dispensational premils so confidently expect, contradict some Scriptural teachings. I close this chapter with a summary of the reasons why the church of Jesus Christ should not expect the millennium as taught by dispensational and "classical" premillennialists.

- Millennialists get their picture of what the millennium will look like from Old Testament prophecies, and their time-frame—the thousand years—from Revelation 20. The combination of these two sources is arbitrary. The promises of the Old Testament say nothing about the thousand years and Revelation 20:1-10 says absolutely nothing about Israel, Jerusalem, an earthly kingdom of Jesus, or a temple.

- Revelation 20:1-10 remains a puzzling passage. Even the best equipped and careful interpreter cannot solemnly swear that he or she is absolutely sure what it means. Therefore the church of Christ should not derive new doctrines, such as multiple resurrections and multiple judgments, from this passage. Such doctrines are not taught by, and may even contradict, the rest of the New Testament.

- The dispensationalists teach a millennium that is a Jewish theocracy: King David's Son will be enthroned in earthly Jerusalem. The temple will be restored and the Old Testament cultus resumed. The "chosen people" are of Jewish blood and live on Israeli soil. However, such a state of affairs would be a significant reversal of the theological trends in the New Testament (see ch. 8 and 9).

- The New Testament clearly states that the purpose of the second coming of Christ is to complete the work of his first coming. But what could possibly be the purpose of the thousand years? Irenaeus said it was to make us perfect, and the present-day dispensationalists say that Israel must have its glory time on earth. However, there are no such promises or expectations in the New Testament. Jesus and Paul have taught us that "the age to come" has broken into this "present age," which is passing. We eagerly wait for the fullness of the age to come. An extra thousand years of human history that is better than the present age but inferior to the age to come makes no biblical sense.

- Similarly, why should Christ, who won the victory by his death and resurrection and was crowned as victor in his ascension, have to fight two more battles—one at the beginning and one at the end of the thousand years—before he is recognized as Lord of all? Does he not already have authority over all things right now? And why should glorified and perfect people have to return from the joy of their Master to live in a blemished world with ordinary people in the flesh, people who marry and give in marriage and bear children. . . . The perfect would then have to live with the imperfect, the sinful with the sinless. Thousands, even millions of people would be converted. Yet sinfulness would increase, and at the end of the thousand years Satan would lead a worldwide rebellion against Christ. This scheme does not fit the biblical frame of salvation history. What the premils expect has not been promised in the Bible and cannot be harmonized with it.

THE MILLENNIUM IN CHURCH HISTORY

The Early Church

The ancient church was a persecuted church. Early Christians kept one eye on the sky, awaiting the Lord's return. At the same time, they kept their other eye on Rome, the enemy of Christ. They expected the Antichrist, whose number is 666 (Rev. 13:11-18). They were sure he *had* to be a Roman emperor.

Premillennialists give the impression that their teaching was the normal, orthodox faith of the early church until the time of Augustine, and that this truth was partly recovered in Reformation times and fully restored in the nineteenth century.

For instance, Lewis Sperry Chafer, founder of Dallas Theological Seminary, writes, "In the period immediately following the Apostolic Age . . . there is clear evidence of premillennial faith as the normal orthodox position of the church" (*Systematic Theology,* p. 369). The "clear evidence" comes from George N. H. Peters (1825-1909), an obscure Lutheran pastor/author who wrote an exhaustive work on predictive prophecy. His book, *The Theocratic Kingdom,* was originally published in 1844. Chafer accepts as a premillennialist every early Christian writer named by Peters. But even a quick reading of Barnabas shows that his "millennium" is nothing other than the eternal Sabbath.

Justin Martyr is premil, but he acknowledges that "Many who belong to the pure and pious faith and are Christians think otherwise" (*Dialogue with Trypho*—see also Stanley J. Grenz, *The Millennial Maze.* His second chapter gives a nice summary of "Millenarianism in the History of the Church").

Irenaeus was also a premillennialist. However, modern premils should be careful not to appropriate him as one of their own. He does not deal with the millennium as a topic by itself. He writes against the gnostics and their antimaterialism. Most of his writing is taken up by a defense of the resurrection of our bodies. And when he gets to the millennium (*Against Heresies,* Book 5, xxxii-xxxvi), his main concern remains the reliability of the literal promise. But Irenaeus's identification of the earthly kingdom of the saints gathered in the restored Jerusalem includes the church of Christ (xxxiv). That's why D. H. Kromminga loved Irenaeus's writing so much: here he found a pillar in the church who believed in one covenant of grace throughout the Scriptures and yet also taught a millennium on earth before the final judgment. Irenaeus was Kromminga's soulmate, "a covenantal millennialist" (foreword to *The Millennium*).

Irenaeus, bishop of Lyons (about A.D. 185), taught that the word *Lateinos* in its Greek spelling has the numerical value of 666. It is the name for Rome, the last of the four kingdoms in Daniel. "The Latins are they who at present bear rule," he added. But he also suggested that the Greek spelling of Titan (*teitan*) added up to 666. He found that name particularly fitting for the soon-to-come Antichrist. But he restrained himself. If God had wanted us to know the name he would have told John when he gave him the vision, not very long ago, "almost in our day, towards the end of the reign of Domitian" (*Against Heresies,* Book 5, ch. xxx).

During the Constantinian Era

The church's outlook changed when the Roman emperor was no longer the church's enemy but became its protector and promoter, beginning with Constantine the Great, who was emperor from A.D. 306 to A.D. 337. The fervent expectation of the Lord's return and of the millennium waned. So did the fearful expectation of the Antichrist.

Augustine (A.D. 354-430) also contributed to the decline of millennial fervor. Augustine was bishop of Hippo in Algeria, North Africa. After the apostles themselves, he was the most influential teacher in the Western church. In discussing Revelation 20 (*The City of God,* Book xx, ch. 7), he recalls the old arguments for the millennium as a literal thousand-year Sabbath rest, comparable to God's rest after the six days of creation. He neither supports nor denies the argument, but admits "I myself at one time accepted such an opinion." He writes that people may believe that the saints will rise to a millennium of delight in God's company, as long as that prospect involves something other, something more spiritual than gorging oneself on heaps of food and drink. He prefers to take the thousand years to represent "all the years of the Christian era, a perfect number being used to indicate the 'fullness of time.'"

Augustine believed in and taught two resurrections—the one spiritual (baptism or rebirth), and the other corporeal. A person may escape the second death (eternal punishment) if he or she has part in the first resurrection (Rev. 20:6). For Augustine, the binding of Satan happened when Jesus began to free us from the prison of Satan at his first coming (Matt. 12:29). At the end of the Christian era, Satan will be loosed for three and one-half years to show all his evil power and conquer those who are not real Christians.

The main outline of Augustine's teachings about the millennium has been widely accepted in the church until today. But there are also points in his teaching about Revelation 20 that nobody accepts. He says, for example, that Satan being chained in the abyss means that, shut out from believing hearts, "he has taken still deeper hold upon unbelievers." The abyss stands for the collective heart of unbelievers. Augustine's identification of the kingdom of heaven with the church in the world became official doctrine of the Roman Catholic Church. They agree with Augustine in contending that the thrones John saw in Revelation 20:4 are occupied by the prelates "who govern the Church here and now" (Book xx, ch. 9).

From the Middle Ages Until Now

- The Roman Catholic Church had no place for a millennial kingdom, since the kingdom was already here in the church. Yet, during the medieval period, many people believed that the kingdom would be truly revealed if the church were to be purified by the power of the Holy Spirit. So whenever there was an expectation of the millennial kingdom during the Middle Ages, it was accompanied by the expectation of a new outpouring of the Spirit. In the thirteenth century, Joachim of Fiore expected the new era to dawn when the spirituality of certain new orders of monks or nuns would diffuse into the land.

- In the fourteenth century, when the pope of Rome was opposed by an anti-pope in Avignon, John Wycliffe predicted that the purification of the church would involve the removal of the powers that kept the Bible from the people. His vision became the conviction of the Reformers.

- In general, the Reformers stuck to the Augustinian understanding of Revelation 20. But they considered the institution of the papacy to be the anti-Christian power that blocked the reform of the church. However, among the Protestants, extremist Anabaptists still expected to see an outpouring of the Spirit accompanied by the establishment of Christ's millennial reign.

- The Church of England, though it had severed its tie with the pope of Rome, still retained many papal practices. According to the Puritans, these remnants of the old bondage had to be removed before the millennial glory of Christ would be seen on the earth. It was among the English and later the American Puritans that millennial thinking revived. The Puritans knew that God worked through human agents and they willingly offered themselves to take away the government from Christ's opponents. In the middle of the seventeenth century, they called themselves the "Fifth Monarchy Men," a term based on Daniel 2 and 7. Daniel prophesies that when the four "monarchies," the kingdoms of the Babylonians, the Medo-Persians, the Greeks, and the Romans are smashed, "a kingdom that will never be destroyed" (2:44) will be established. This is the Fifth Monarchy. These Puritan volunteers supported Oliver Cromwell in the hope that they could bring the millennial kingdom of Christ to England.

- As I mentioned earlier, millennialism flourished in America as well. It arrived from Britain as "The Puritan Hope" (see the book so titled, written by Iain H. Murray). This optimism in the sure expectation of the victory of the gospel and the conversion of the world received its own American character during the Great Awakening of the 1740s. Jonathan Edwards (1703-1758) thought that the revivals marked the beginning of the final phase of God's work. "The victory of God's people could not be far in the future" (Stanley J. Grenz, *The Millennial Maze*, p. 56). Grenz calls Edwards the father of American postmillennialism. However, according to George M. Marsden (*Fundamentalism and American Culture*, p. 240), "clear distinctions in terminology between 'premillennial' and 'postmillennial' do not seem to occur before the nineteenth century." Marsden observes that the label *amillennial* was not used until the twentieth century.

- The main tenor of postmillennialism is attractive to all who love the Lord and his kingdom. It advances the idea that, by God's Word and Spirit, all opposition to Jesus Christ will be broken, and all tribes and nations will be Christianized. In the eighteenth century, the Calvinists of Britain and America were nearly unanimous in this optimistic faith. Missions flourished and comprehensive plans were made to cover the whole earth with the preaching of the gospel. Iain Murray contends that the funeral of C. H. Spurgeon (February 1892) marks the end of this era.

- The change came through Edward Irving (1792-1834) and John Nelson Darby (1800-1882). We've already examined Darby's system, canonized by the *Scofield Reference Bible*. Irving is less familiar to the American evangelicals. Yet, "all the salient features of Darby's scheme are to be found in Irving" (Iain H. Muray, *Puritan Hope*, p. 200). Generally speaking, the millennialism of the nineteenth century offered the optimistic hope that "from ocean unto ocean, our land shall own you Lord, and, filled with true devotion, obey your sovereign Word" (Robert Murray, 1880). This was the postmil expectation of a golden age of a Christianized world after which the Lord would return. But in the twentieth century, J. N. Darby's dispensationalism and premillennialism took center stage in many regions.

- The difference between the postmillennial expectation and the premillennial outlook is strikingly clear from a speech on the "Progress of Evil on the Earth," which Darby gave in Geneva in 1840. Addressing the Calvinists in Calvin's old city, he stated, "What we are about to consider will tend to shew that, instead of permitting ourselves to hope for a continued progress of good, we must expect a progress of evil; and that the hope of the earth being filled with the knowledge of the Lord before the exercise of His judgment . . . is delusive . . ." (Darby, quoted by Iain Murray, *Puritan Hope,* p. 201). According to postmillennialism, things will get better and better, but according to premillennialism, things will go from bad to worse to the final calamity. The premillennial prophecy of an increasing falling away from the faith and an ever more powerful revelation of worldwide evil is familiar to everyone who listens to contemporary premil television preachers.

- I'll close this brief survey by observing that the Darby-Scofield tradition, which has been getting center-stage attention in North America for the last forty years, is now being revised by the schools that promoted it. In the 1990s scholars at Dallas Theological Seminary are writing books that call into question the most characteristic thesis of the Darby-Scofield system, namely the fundamental distinction they make between God's purposes for the church and for the Jews. Dispensationalism is being rethought. See, for example, Craig A. Blaising and Darrell L. Block's *Progressive Dispensationalism.*

- We seem to have some reason, finally, to hope for a greater consensus regarding our view of the end times. Perhaps, after more books and more conferences, we may reach a basic agreement on what the Bible teaches us about the future. But it will be a long time before this new and scholarly reflection will have a noticeable influence on the television preachers who remain so fiercely dogmatic about their interpretation of prophecy.

Jesus Christ

—Sir Anthony Van Dyck, 1599-1641

CHAPTER 8

ISRAEL, CHRIST, AND THE CHURCH

Two events have made the discussion of the relationship between the Jews and the Christian church unavoidable. The first is the murder of more than five million Jews by Nazi Germany from 1939-1945. That slaughter has overwhelmed Christians with guilt feelings.

In some instances this sense of remorse is not well-placed. Nazi Germans also murdered members of my family. My wife and I belong to clans that resisted the Nazis and risked execution by hiding Jews and others the Nazis wanted to kill. But I do recognize that a thousand years of anti-Jewish preaching and practice preceded the Holocaust.

This millennium began with the crusades aimed at freeing "the holy land" from the Muslims. The crusaders believed that the Jews, whom they called "Christ-killers," were as worthy of death as the Muslims. During the Middle Ages, the church kept alive this hatred against Jews and Turks. In the year 1215, Pope Innocent III made the Jews wear the "yellow badge." And from then on, all over Europe, Jews lived in ghettoes.

The Reformation brought some oases of religious toleration, for example, the Netherlands. But it also brought further oppression through the unholy wedding of church and state. In Luther's Germany and in the pope's Italy and Spain, anti-Jewish sentiments flourished. Therefore, as members of the Christian church with roots in Western Europe, we must admit that centuries of unenlightened, ill-informed church talk about the Jews made Hitler's crime possible.

Mission to the Jews?

The guilt and shame about the Holocaust has been so severe among Christians that after Auschwitz all mainline churches "have come to repudiate mission to the Jews, even if they have not justified this by adequate doctrinal explanations" (Gregory Baum, quoted by Richard R. De Ridder in *God Has Not Rejected His People*, p. 69). De Ridder himself issues a strong summons to bring the gospel of Christ to the Jews. And the Roman Catholic Church, represented by the Second Vatican Council in 1965, issued statements that were "as clear a condemnation of this church's past behavior to the Jews . . . [and] as near a repudiation of past doctrine concerning [the Jews] as a church claiming infallibility could go" (H. L. Ellison, *The Mystery of Israel*, p. 9).

The father of Isaac C. Rottenberg was a Christian Jew who "shared his faith with his people, and during the Holocaust he shared their fate in the Nazi ovens" ("Should There Be a Christian Witness to the Jews?" *The Christian Century,* April 13, 1977). Rottenberg, a minister in the Reformed Church in America, objects to a triumphalistic mission of the church aimed at converting Jews without awareness of the need to convert the church. He favors *witness* in a Christian-Jewish dialogue, rather than *mission.*

The positive result of renewed reflection by Christians has been a fresh recognition of the Jewishness of our Bible and of Jesus himself. Throughout the Christian church "after Auschwitz," one may sense a humbler attitude and greater love even towards those Jews who do not yet believe in their Messiah.

The Political State of Israel

The second event that has forced the Christian church to spell out its relationship to the Jews is the founding of the independent state of Israel on May 14, 1948. Premillennialists had predicted that someday the Jews would return to Palestine. When it really happened, they ranked the good news of the formation of the Jewish state second only to the return of Christ himself (John Hagee, *Beginning of the End,* p. 92). Indeed, ever since the Jewish state was formed, an avalanche of books, films, videotapes, and sermons tell us that we are the last generation to live on this planet before the Lord returns.

The rebirth of Israel was the keystone of Hal Lindsey's bestseller and of numerous other books and tapes that outlined God's "program." The premils caught the attention of North America with their message: All that you see happening in the world today has been predicted in the Bible, therefore listen to the Bible and its prophecy experts. Today we have premil preachers who give us chapter and verse for every political occurrence in Europe and the Middle East. And when they are wrong—for example, about the empire of the Soviet Union, which unexpectedly collapsed, and about the West European Union, which has fourteen "kings," not ten—their listeners easily forgive and soon forget.

Israel and the Church of Christ: Three Views

There are three different views on the relationship between Israel and the church of Christ:

- The dispensational Darby-Scofield tradition teaches that God has one plan for Israel and another for the church. Israel will get land and a literal kingdom in an earthly Jerusalem under the government of King Jesus, who will rule from David's earthly throne. The church gets a heavenly kingdom, a heavenly king, and a heavenly inheritance. God's program for Israel and God's program for the church have little to do with each other. When God is finished with the church age, he raptures the true church and returns to his kingdom for Israel. Israel and the church travel on parallel tracks.

- The Augustinian and Roman Catholic traditions hold that the church has taken the place of Israel in the New Testament. All Israel's privileges now belong to the church. When the track for the church was laid, the Israel program was obliterated.

- The Reformed tradition focuses on Jesus as the One who fulfills the role of Israel. He is the true Son of David and the Seed of Abraham. In him Israel is restored and Gentiles are incorporated. Jews reach completion when they know their Messiah, and Gentiles become part of Israel when they believe in Jesus. The track laid by God in choosing Abraham has now become a highway on which all nations (should) travel.

The two-track view of the dispensationalists is now in trouble. Bible scholars in many dispensationalist schools and seminaries don't wish to be represented any longer by their popularizer, Hal Lindsey. "Progressive dispensationalists" are open to a serious conversation with those who hold to a covenantal ("one-track") way of Bible reading (see *Christianity Today*, Sept. 12, 1994). But it will take awhile before we find this less dogmatic dispensationalism on television.

The second approach, where the Israel track is erased and the church takes over, is universally suspect. Those who hold this view have a well-deserved guilt complex. This view has led Christians to think of themselves as superior to the Jews, and that attitude has bred contempt for the Jews.

The third approach, which has a Reformed understanding of the relationship between the Old and the New Testament, is gaining ground. It teaches that the whole Bible is the history of one covenant of grace that God made with his one people. This one covenant is progressively unfolded through two dispensations, the old and the new. The new dispensation is the completion of the old. And the one Mediator is Jesus.

The Covenant with Abraham

In the first eleven chapters of Genesis, we read of God's dealings with the whole world. But in Genesis 12, God calls one couple and their (future) children to be his special people. To Abraham God said, "You are my covenant partner, your friends are my friends, your enemies are my enemies." Yet God did not forget all the other nations of the world. On the contrary, God called Abraham to be a blessing to the world (v. 2), and God promised that all peoples on earth would receive the blessing now given to Abraham (v. 3):

¹The LORD had said to Abram, "Leave your country, your people, and your father's household and go to the land I will show you.

[2]I will make you into a great nation and I will bless you; I will make your name great, and you will be a blessing. [3]I will bless those who bless you, and whoever curses you I will curse; and all peoples on earth will be blessed through you."

—Genesis 12:1-3

Today the important question is, Who are the blessed children of Abraham? The question is immediately relevant to more than two billion people, because all Jews, Muslims, and Christians claim Abraham as their father and Abraham's special blessing as their inheritance.

Dispensationalism claims that the children of Abraham are the ethnic Israelites, arguing that we must not spiritualize God's promises. Therefore Abraham's land

---

Dispensationalists quote God's words in Genesis 12:3 and apply them to the state of Israel. Whoever is kind to Israelis will be blessed by God, and whoever opposes them will meet God as an enemy. Or, as John Hagee puts it, "What a nation or an individual does to the nation of Israel is what God repays to them. God could not have been more clear: 'I will bless those who bless you, and I will curse him who curses you'" (*Beginning of the End,* p. 180).

This understanding of God's friendship with Abraham has made evangelical Christians in North America put pressure on their government and on their Christian friends to "bless" the state of Israel with political and financial favors. Mike Evans, one of the greatest promotors of Christian friendship for political Israel, called the state of Israel "America's key to survival." He meant that God would destroy the U.S.A. if it failed to support Israel. Another organization of "Friends of Israel," headed by Jack Hayward and Pat Boone, collects money to relocate Jewish people from the former Soviet Union to Israel—not to bring them the gospel, but to bring them "home."

During the Old Testament, it was indeed the case that God would curse whoever cursed the children of Abraham and bless those who blessed them. Therefore the Amalekites had to be annihilated (Exod. 17:8-15; 1 Sam. 15), but Rahab and all who favored God's people were blessed. During the Old Testament dispensation, one's relationship to God depended on one's relationship to the children of Abraham.

Not so today. There is not one nation—not the United States, not Canada, and not the state of Israel—of which God has said: "Your friend is my friend and your enemy is my enemy." Our relationship to God is not determined by what we do to Israel. Everyone's relationship to God depends on his or her relationship to Christ. Whoever curses this Son of Abraham shall be cursed. But whoever blesses him shall be blessed.

goes to Abraham's children, meaning ethnic Jews. The formation of the state of Israel is God's work. God has begun to fulfill the *unconditional* promise to Abraham: "To your descendants I give this land, from the river of Egypt to the great river, the Euphrates . . ." (Gen. 15:18; see, for example, John F. Walvoord, *Israel in Prophecy*). They do not deny, however, that through Jesus Christ many spiritual blessings have come from Abraham to the Gentile Christians.

The Bible gives no simple answer to the question of who the children of Abraham are. In the first place, "not all Israelites truly belong to Israel, and not all of Abraham's children are his true descendants," as Paul observed (Rom. 9:6-7, NRSV). The principle of election is at work in Abraham's history. The blessing and the promise go to Isaac and not to Ishmael, they go to Jacob and not to Esau. God's sovereign freedom determines that choice. And Abraham's children must be counted according to God's choice, not ours.

Besides, God's wrath against the sinful rebellion of Israel cut off numerous branches and individuals: "For forty years I was angry with that generation. . . . So I declared on oath in my anger, 'They shall never enter my rest'" (Ps. 95:10-11). As a matter of fact, the people of Israel who were formed as a nation when God delivered them from slavery (Exod. 20:2) were finally given up to slavery in Assyria and Babylonia by their angry God.

These two principles, God's freedom to choose and human responsibility to trust and obey, should make us very careful not to teach that promises to Abraham are "unconditional," as dispensationalist Christians do.

God did not forget his promises to Abraham, but these were only for a *remnant* of Israel. And the word *remnant* tells of justice: it's all that remains after God has punished the nation. *Remnant* also speaks of mercy, for if there were no forgiveness, no one would remain. Isaiah prophesies, "A remnant will return, a remnant of Jacob will return to the Mighty God. Though your people, O Israel, be like the sand by the sea, only a remnant will return" (Isa. 10:21-22).

God must be praised that a remnant escaped Israel's deserved punishment: "Who is a God like you, who pardons sin and forgives the transgression of the remnant of his inheritance? . . . You will be true to Jacob, and show mercy to Abraham, as you pledged on oath to our fathers in days long ago" (Mic. 7:18-20).

Already in the Old Testament it is far too simple to say that an ethnic Jew, simply because he is an ethnic Jew, is an heir to the promises made to Abraham.

The Covenant with Abraham in the New Testament

In the New Testament dispensation, no doubt exists about the validity of the covenant with Abraham. The big question is, Who are the children of Abraham?

A claim that one is born of a Jewish mother is certainly not enough to inherit the blessings of Abraham. When John the Baptizer warns Israel that the kingdom is near and that, therefore, all must repent, he adds, "And do not think that you can say to yourselves, 'We have Abraham as our father.' I tell you that out of these stones God can raise up children for Abraham" (Matt. 3:9).

Jesus himself often speaks of Abraham and the desire of the Jews to give themselves legal standing before God by calling themselves children of Abraham. The most scathing remarks are found in John 8, where Jesus says, in effect, "If you are of the mind of Abraham you would rejoice to see me; if you were children of God you would love me; but because you are the brood of the devil you want to kill me."

Paul has different ways of saying who the children of Abraham are. In Romans 4:9-12 he says something that must have sounded revolutionary to Jewish ears. Abraham, he asserts, is the father of the uncircumcised (Gentiles) who believe—just as Abraham himself believed when he was still uncircumcised. Paul means that Abraham's faith was credited to him as righteousness (see Gen. 15:6) and that circumcision was not instituted until later (Gen. 17:10). Paul adds that Abraham is also the father of the circumcised (Jews), but only insofar as they believe as Abraham did. Abraham is the father of *believers!*

In Galations 3 we find Paul's clearest and most memorable answer to the question, Who inherits the blessings of Abraham?

> [8]The Scripture foresaw that God would justify the Gentiles by faith, and announced the gospel in advance to Abraham: "All nations will be blessed through you." [9]So those who have faith are blessed along with Abraham, the man of faith. . . . [13]Christ redeemed us from the curse of the law by becoming a curse for us, for it is written: "Cursed is everyone who is hung on a tree." [14]He redeemed us in order that the blessing given to Abraham might come to the Gentiles through Christ Jesus, so that by faith we might receive the promise of the Spirit.
>
> [26]You are all sons of God through faith in Christ Jesus, [27]for all of you who were baptized into Christ have clothed yourselves with Christ. [28]There is neither Jew nor Greek, slave nor free, male nor female, for you are all one in Christ Jesus. [29]If you belong to Christ, then you are Abraham's seed, and heirs according to the promise.
>
> —Galatians 3:8-9, 13-14, 26-29

In verse 8, Paul deals directly with Genesis 12:1-3. There, he says, God already proclaimed the gospel, because in that passage God promised that the blessing of his covenant would be extended to the Gentiles.

Well, then, how does this blessing of Abraham come to the Gentiles? The Gentiles were always under the curse and not under the blessing. However, that curse has now been removed. It was laid on Jesus: "Cursed is everyone who is hung on a tree" (v. 13). Through the accursed death of "the Seed," "the Son," "the Offspring" of Abraham, the blessing of God has come to the Gentiles. Not only the Gentiles, but all who believe as Abraham believed are blessed along with Abraham.

Thus Paul answers the burning question of the New Testament—Who are the children of Abraham?—with this one, short, classic statement: "If you belong to Christ, then you are Abraham's seed, and heirs according to the promise" (Gal. 3:29). You have to belong to Jesus Christ to be the heir of Abraham.

Jews and Gentiles, circumcised and uncircumcised, must all, by faith, belong to Christ, be baptized into Christ, and be clothed with Christ. And when they are thus united with him, something happens in their relationship to God and in their relationship to one another. They receive the blessings of God. They receive the forgiveness of sin and are made heirs of life everlasting. The old differences that set them apart from one another are no longer important: "There is neither Jew nor Greek, slave nor free, male nor female" (v. 28). What used to determine their personal and group identity is now, at best, a minor distinction.

"I am a Jew," one would say, and that would summarize all of his privileges, obligations, and way of life. "I am a slave" another would say, and that one statement determined his status, role, behavior, and lot. "I am a woman," yet another would say, and that fairly well summed up what she could do and what she could not do, what she was and what she could never be. But now every one of them can say: "I belong to Christ!" From now on that reality determines the basic identity of the Jew, the Gentile, the slave, the free, the woman, and the man. It spells out their basic unity and sameness. It determines their privileges and obligations, what they are and what they are going to be, how they should behave and how they may never conduct themselves.

Jesus introduced a new mode of living. It is no longer important where one comes from, only where one is: *in* Christ or *outside of* Christ. *In Christ* all of us share in a new reality. We are children of God, brothers and sisters to each other. The old is past, the new has already begun.

From the Many to the One, from the One to the Many

Messiah Jesus fulfills the role of Israel. He becomes the blessing to the world. And our attitude to Jesus determines whether or not we are a part of God's people. By accepting Jesus we are "in," by rejecting him we are "out."

This story is at the heart of the New Testament. It is explicitly taught or clearly implied in the gospels and the other writings. (A full treatment of this topic is impossible within the scope of this book. For a recent book on this subject written from a Reformed point of view, see David E. Holwerda's book, *Jesus and Israel, One Covenant or Two?*)

God wanted his people to be obedient and to be a blessing to the world. That was God's intention in calling Abraham, and that was God's will throughout the history of Israel. That's why God named Israel his beloved son who was called out of Egypt (Hos. 11:1), his servant, appointed to be a light for the Gentiles through whom salvation would be brought to the ends of the earth (Isa. 49:6). For forty years God tested and trained Israel to "teach (him) that man does not live on bread alone but on every word that comes from the mouth of the LORD" (Deut. 8:3).

Israel was disobedient and failed in its mission. But then Jesus came as the beloved Son (Matt. 3:17) called out of Egypt (Matt. 2:15), who wandered in the desert for forty days and learned that "Man does not live on bread alone, but on every word that comes from the mouth of God" (Matt. 4:4). It is not a nation, but one person, who is "a light for revelation to the Gentiles," according to the prophetic words of Simeon (Luke 2:32).

Jesus is corporate Israel. All that Israel was intended to be was fulfilled by the One. He is also the One into whom the many are incorporated. Through him, Israel is reborn, renewed, regathered. He rebuilds Israel on twelve apostles, paralleling the twelve patriarchs. Old Simeon had said that "falling and rising" in Israel would be caused by Jesus (Luke 2:34). As a matter of fact, Christ has become the stone on which people are either built as living stones into the new temple of God, or they fall over this stone and are lost (1 Pet. 2:4-8).

Those who believe and are built on Jesus inherit all the lofty titles of God's Israel: "a chosen people, a royal priesthood, a holy nation" (1 Pet. 2:9, quoting Exod. 19:5-6, the covenant formula at Sinai). It's not *as if* they are Israel, but they *are* God's Israel. Many who are addressed in Peter's letter came from Gentile nations. This is evident because Peter says of them that they inherited "the empty way of life" from their ancestors (1:18). But their incorporation had been prophesied (Hos. 1:9-10; Isa. 44:5; 1 Pet. 2:10) and is effected in Christ.

Not only the titles of Israel but also the role of Israel belongs to this people. From now on, their goal in life is, "that you may declare the praises of him who called you out of darkness into his wonderful light" (1 Pet. 2:9). Israel was to be God's lightbearer in the world (Isa. 49:6). Jesus fulfilled that calling and became "a light for revelation to the Gentiles" (Luke 2:32). In fact, he became "the light of the world" (John 8:12). But Christ also appointed his followers to be "the light of the world" (Matt. 5:14). Thus the ancient assignment to be "a light for the Gentiles" and to "bring salvation to the ends of the earth" is fulfilled in those who carry the gospel of Jesus Christ to the countries of the world (Acts 13:47).

The calling of the many (Israel) is fulfilled in the One (Christ), and the calling of the One (Christ) is effected through the many (Christ's church). Israel, Christ, and the church form only a single people of God.

The Day of Judgment

—Hartmann Schedel, 1440-1514

CHAPTER 9

THE NEW COVENANT

In the last chapter we saw that the calling of the many (Israel) is fulfilled in the One (Christ), and the calling of the One (Christ) is effected through the many (Christ's church). I concluded that Israel, Christ, and the church form only a single people of God. If this is so, what does this mean for the covenant relationship God established with Israel? Is that covenant still in effect? If so, how?

A New Covenant with an Ancient People

God's people of the New Testament are not a new Israel. There is only one Israel, one people of God. But God made a new covenant with this ancient people. The classic text for the prophecy of the new covenant is Jeremiah 31:31-34.

> [31]"The time is coming," declares the LORD, "when I will make a new covenant with the house of Israel and with the house of Judah. [32]It will not be like the covenant I made with their forefathers when I took them by the hand to lead them out of Egypt, because they broke my covenant, though I was a husband to them," declares the LORD. [33]"This is the covenant I will make with the house of Israel after that time," declares the LORD. "I will put my law in their minds and write it on their hearts. I will be their God, and they will be my people. [34]No longer will a man teach his neighbor, or a man his brother, saying 'Know the LORD,' because they will all know me, from the least of them to the greatest," declares the LORD. "For I will forgive their wickedness and will remember their sins no more."
>
> —Jeremiah 31:31-34

The new covenant replaces the one God made with Israel "when [the LORD] took them by the hand to lead them out of Egypt" (v. 32). That refers to the Sinai covenant.

The first thing that is new in the new covenant is that the law is in the hearts and minds of the people. The stubborn disobedience has ended and by inner compulsion people want to do what God's law requires. This refers to the end-time gift of the Holy Spirit. Paul calls himself and his coworkers "ministers of a new covenant" (2 Cor. 3:6), and he describes the Corinthian converts as people who have God's writing "not with ink but with the Spirit of the living God, not on tablets of stone but on tablets of human hearts" (v. 3).

The second thing that is new in the new covenant is the universal knowledge of God—a time in which mediators are no longer necessary. God's people won't be saying to each other: "'Know the Lord,' because they will all know me from the least of them to the greatest" (v. 34). This too refers to the indwelling Spirit, who teaches young and old, the simplest and the wisest, to say "Abba, Father." Therefore John writes to children, fathers, and young people that they share in the forgiveness of sins, have overcome the evil one, and are strong in the knowledge of the Lord. "You have an anointing from the Holy One, and all of you know the truth" (1 John 2:20).

And how is this indwelling of the Holy One possible in the sinful people under the new covenant? What is the basis of the new covenant? "I will forgive their wickedness and will remember their sins no more" (Jer. 31:34). This refers to the once-for-all, complete forgiveness of all our sins through the atoning death of our Lord Jesus Christ. We remember, believe, and celebrate this fact whenever we lift up the cup of the new covenant in his blood (see Mark.14:24; Luke 22:20; 1 Cor. 11:25).

The epistle to the Hebrews makes this new covenant the centerpiece of the passage we find in chapters 8 through 10. It quotes the whole Jeremiah passage in 8:8-12, and partly again in 10:16-17. The truth of the whole argument in Hebrews depends on the fact that the old Sinai covenant has been replaced by the new covenant through the death of Christ.

Is the New Covenant in Force?

Our dispensationalist friends teach that the new covenant will come into force *some day,* when God visits the Jews in Palestine. The church has already received some spiritual benefits from the new covenant, they admit, because we are already blessed by Christ's atoning death. But the new covenant must be made with the literal "house of Israel and with the house of Judah," that is, with those who can trace their bloodline to Jacob, the grandson of Abraham (see the *New Scofield Study Bible,* notes on Jer. 31:31 and Heb. 8:8; Lewis Sperry Chafer, *Systematic Theology, II,* pp. 416-418; J. Dwight Pentecost, *Thy Kingdom Come,* ch. 15; and John F. Walvoord, *Israel in Prophecy,* ch. 3).

I am not the only one who is somewhat perplexed by this evasion of what seems to be a very clear teaching of the New Testament. Albertus Pieters, who used to be a professor of Bible and Missions at Western Theological Seminary of the Reformed Church in America, has done an older and excellent biblical study of this issue, *The Seed of Abraham.* Speaking of the replacement of the old by the new covenant, he leads his readers through the argument of the letter to the Hebrews. Then he exclaims:

> Now, believe it or not, there are honored brethren, learned in the Scriptures, declaring themselves ready to accept what the word of God teaches, who can read these chapters and still think that the

New Covenant spoken of by Jeremiah the prophet has not yet come to pass; but must be set up in the end-time, not with us but with the remnant of Israel after the flesh! I know of many marvels in Bible study, but of nothing more marvelous than this.

—p. 68

How is it possible to maintain a dispensationalist position on the new covenant after reading and believing the epistle to the Hebrews, 2 Corinthians 3, and celebrating the Lord's Supper to the praise of "Jesus, the mediator of a new covenant"?

What makes such a thing possible is a stubborn commitment to the theory that comes from John Nelson Darby in the 1830s that asserts that God has one program for the church, another one for Israel, and that these two are never the same.

Jeremiah predicted that God would make the new covenant with "the house of Israel and with the house of Judah" (31:31). These terms were remarkable already at that time, because *Israel,* the Northern kingdom of ten tribes, did not really exist anymore. The capital of Israel, Samaria, was destroyed, and the people taken away in 721 B.C. Jeremiah lived to see the fall of Jerusalem in 586 B.C., that is, 135 years later. So the term "house of Israel and house of Judah" means that God would remember *all* of his people. God would make a new covenant with the remnant of his ancient nation.

And so he did. In the night in which he was betrayed, Christ gave them the bread as his body and when he gave them the wine he said, "This cup is the new covenant in my blood, which is poured out for you" (Luke 22:20). These were his twelve (Jewish) disciples, who formed the foundation on which Christ rebuilt God's people Israel. Jesus mediated God's covenant with the remnant of Israel.

In dispensationalist literature, writers constantly distinguish between "Israel" and "the church." Since 1945, in conversations with the Jews, we constantly speak of "Jews" and "Christians." But these are false contrasts. All the first Christians were Jews. At one point the church was only made up of Jews. And when the first Gentiles entered, the question of whether these Gentiles should be circumcised (Acts 15) had to be answered. As Leslie Newbigin observed, the very fact that this question could be raised shows that neither side in the controversy doubted that the church of Christ was the Israel of God (*The Reunion of the Church*, p. 31, as quoted by Pieters, *The Seed of Abraham*, p. 62).

The new covenant has been established with the remnant of Israel. They who now live under the sprinkled blood of Christ *are* the Israel of the new covenant.

The Gospel Is the Equalizer

After the death and resurrection of Christ, God stretched out his arms to all races on the globe in order to unite them in Christ. Before that time, he allowed them to live in ignorance. "In the past God overlooked such ignorance, but now he commands all people everywhere to repent" (Acts 17:30). It is no accident that on the day of Pentecost more than fifteen groups and nations are mentioned who heard the works of God proclaimed in their own tongue. After Pentecost the disastrous divisions of Babel (see Gen. 11) are going to be healed by the gospel of Christ and the power from heaven.

The mission after Pentecost is aimed at all nations. And the gospel message equalizes all people. The gospel first declares that all people, Jews and Gentiles alike, are under the power of sin and deserve the just condemnation of God (Rom. 1:18-3:20). It goes on to say that the way to be right with God "comes through faith in Jesus Christ to all who believe. There is no difference, for all have sinned and fall short of the glory of God, and are justified freely by his grace through the redemption that came by Christ Jesus" (Rom. 3:22-24).

The gospel attacks the pride and prejudice that separate clans, races, and nations from each other. The gospel makes us equal—all have sinned, all need Christ—and it reunites us in the second Adam (Rom. 5).

When Christ had fulfilled his earthly mission, God began to remove the sinful divisions that have so painfully divided this suffering world. God also began to remove the deepest division in humanity, the division between Jews and Gentiles. While the other divisions were based on color, language, or other accidents of birth and history, the one between Jews and Gentiles was based on God's election. Yet in Christ, even this division has been overcome. Once we are united with Christ in his death and resurrection "there is neither Jew nor Gentile." Or, as Paul repeats three times, "Circumcision is nothing and uncircumcision is nothing" (1 Cor. 7:19). All that counts is being "a new creation" (Gal. 6:15), "keeping God's commands" (1 Cor. 7:19), and "faith expressing itself through love" (Gal. 5:6). These are the qualities that are valued by God.

No Christian can deny, of course, that this is the progressive history of salvation. Dispensationalist Christians don't deny that either. They say, however, that what the Bible teaches about the unity of races and nations in Christ is true only during the "church age." After this age, and after the seven-year tribulation, we will get the millennium, which will be the age of Israel.

If the dispensationalists are right, the old story of "race and land," or "blood and soil," which lost significance when we were set free by the gospel, will be revived again when God resumes his dealings with Israel. But that would not be progressive salvation history! It would be regressive!

Is this really what we should expect? Is there a biblical promise for a future national Israel?

The promises of a restored nation of Israel and a rebuilt earthly Jerusalem are found only in the Old Testament. Most of these predictions refer to the return following the exile in Babylon. Sometimes these predictions also speak of the end time. One should remember, however, how Old Testament prophets, and perhaps all prophets, express themselves. They speak of the unknown future in terms that are understandable in the present. (See a further discussion of this in the next chapter.)

The New Testament does not predict a future nation of Israel. The subject is not mentioned. But there *is* a word of hope for Israel. In Romans 9-11, Paul writes a whole essay about the role of Israel in God's plan of salvation. Paul does not write it abstractly, as you and I might do on some topics. But he writes with "great sorrow and unceasing anguish" (9:2). He wrestles for the souls of the Israelites, and he pins his hope on God's promise and purpose.

Paul insists that God has not rejected Israel, even though most Israelites are rejecting God's Messiah. A remnant continues to which Paul himself belongs (11:1). That remnant believes the gospel. But the "rest" is hardened. Hardening has a human side. It is disobedience, unwillingness to listen (10:16-21). And it has a divine side. It's punishment of unbelievers. First they don't want to listen, then they cannot hear (11:7-10). However, a spirit of disobedience and a hard heart do not frustrate the redemptive plans of God. When God said, "Let my people go!" and Pharaoh said, "No!" he was still cooperating, involuntarily, in God's plan to make his name great (9:17). And when the good news of the gospel came "first to Israel," and Israel said "No!" God appeared to have a pur-

The dispensationalist Christians who are so sure that God will soon "rapture" his church and then continue his program with the Jews have a strong love for the state of Israel. They admire, support, and visit that country. But I have never heard any of them speak of the state of Israel as Paul spoke of his fellow Jews in Romans 9:1-3 and 10:1. Their preachers make all sorts of prophetic-political statements about the state of Israel and the Middle East. But they do not weep because Israel rejects the Messiah. That's what so bothered the apostle Paul. "They are cut off from Christ," he groaned. "I would be willing to take their place if that could save them."

Israel is one of a number of states that has passed an anti-mission law in order to discourage Christian outreach. And the Israeli courts recognize as a Jew anyone who was born of a Jewish mother. But if a Jew acknowledges that Jesus is the Messiah, he or she is called a Christian and is denied Israeli citizenship. I've never heard the premil television preachers talk about this.

pose in the hardening of Israel: "Because of their transgression, salvation has come to the Gentiles to make Israel envious" (11:11).

And that's not the end of God's purpose. The stream of God's saving grace, which was repelled by the stubborn rock of Israel's unbelief, flowed to the Gentiles and brought healing to them. But this movement must be followed by a countermovement. Aroused by jealousy, Israel may accept the Messiah of God's grace by whom the Gentiles are now blessed. The redemptive movement flows back to Israel via the Gentiles. As a matter of fact, Paul is the apostle to the Gentiles "in the hope that I may somehow arouse my own people to envy and save some of them" (11:14).

So All Israel Will Be Saved

[25]I do not want you to be ignorant of this mystery, brothers, so that you may not be conceited: Israel has experienced a hardening in part until the full number of the Gentiles has come in. [26]And so all Israel will be saved, as it is written: "The deliverer will come from Zion; he will turn godlessness away from Jacob. [27]And this is my covenant with them when I take away their sins."

—Romans 11:25-27

We should not be "ignorant of this mystery," says the apostle. By *mystery* he always means a saving purpose of God that was hidden in God's counsel until it pleased God to reveal it. Now Paul sees and proclaims this purpose of God: the hardening of a part of Israel is not final but is intended to last "until the full number of the Gentiles has come in, and so all Israel will be saved" (vv. 25-26).

This phrase is hard to interpret. Generally there are three ways in which these words of Paul are understood.

The first contends that Paul here predicts a future conversion of Israel, which will take place after God is finished with the Gentiles. However, such a prediction of a future conversion of Jews, apart from and after the Gentiles, does not fit the context of chapters 9 through 11. That idea simply is not found in the text. In the context of those chapters, Paul struggles for Israel's salvation, is willing to be rejected by Christ if that could save them, and spends a great deal of effort to gain a few who are now hardened. All of that tension would now suddenly be resolved by a prediction of a conversion at the end of history.

Besides, Paul does not say that "all Israel will be converted," but that "all Israel will be *saved.*" There's a difference. The text does not speak of an action on the part of Israel but of *God's* ongoing, saving work. And he does not say *then* all Israel will be saved, but *so, in this manner* all Israel will be saved.

A second interpretation, connected with the good name of John Calvin, reads *all Israel* as the totality of all God's people. God brings in the full number of the elect from the Gentiles and in this way all Israel is saved. It makes good sense, but today most interpreters agree that Paul is not using *Israel* here inclusively, referring to the totality of God's people. In this passage, Paul contrasts the historical people of Israel with the Gentiles. *Israel* stands for that part of the Jews who are now hardened in unbelief.

A third interpretation takes "and so all Israel will be saved" to refer to the "full number of elect Jews whom it pleases God to bring into the kingdom throughout the ages until the very day when also the full number of the Gentiles shall have been brought in" (William Hendriksen, *Israel in Prophecy*, p. 49). This is also the view of Herman Bavinck (*The Last Things*, p. 106) and Anthony A. Hoekema: "All Israel [is] the sum total of all the remnants throughout history" (*The Bible and the Future*, p. 145).

The most important question here is whether Paul is saying something with respect to the future, or whether he is speaking of a process that is already underway and will continue to the end. Since he says "and *so* all Israel will be saved," not "and *then* all Israel will be saved," the mystery of which we may not be ignorant concerns not God's *time* but God's *method* of saving "all Israel." That's one very important point to keep in mind.

A Process in Motion

Yet Paul does announce a time limit for the hardening of the "rest" of Israel. It will end when the full number of the Gentiles has come in. And most interpreters add: "and then . . . then it's Israel's turn." But Paul doesn't say that. He states: "and so all Israel will be saved." The emphasis is on the *way* in which "all Israel" comes to share in God's salvation—after a God-intended detour.

The texts from Isaiah 59:20-21 that Paul quotes to bolster our hope for Israel have the same uncertainty. Do they speak of the past or of the future, of Christ's first or second coming?

I don't think Paul was referring to the second coming when he wrote "the deliverer will come from Zion." The future tenses—"the deliverer *will* come and he *will* turn godlessness away"—are in the text of Isaiah. *Isaiah* spoke of the future, not Paul. The reference must be to the Lord's coming in grace to Bethlehem and Golgotha. And the covenant mentioned in verse 27 "is not a covenant yet to be made but the fulfillment of one made long before" (F. F. Bruce, *Romans*, p. 210).

When Paul speaks of the salvation of "all Israel," he refers to a process that is now set in motion. He is not making a prediction of a conversion miracle. The best support for this understanding is in verses 30-32. Paul once again cuts out all possible conceit on the part of the Gentiles—that's how he also started in verse 25—while he restates that his hope for a day of grace for Israel is anchored in the mercies of God.

A Wondrous Interdependence

[30]Just as you who were at one time disobedient to God have now received mercy as a result of their disobedience, [31]so they too have now become disobedient in order that they too may now receive mercy as a result of God's mercy to you. [32]For God has bound all men over to disobedience so that he may have mercy on them all.

—Romans 11:30-32

Paul repeats the wonderful interdependence of the ways in which God comes in grace, first to the Gentiles and then to Israel. That wonderful interdependence was part of the content of the mystery mentioned in verse 25. Gentiles received mercy when Israel fell into disobedience. But as a result of God's compassion, God's grace to disobedient Israel now flows back to them from the Gentiles. Notice that he twice uses the word "now" in verse 31 (the second "now" is omitted in many Greek manuscripts). He speaks of this gracious work of God as an ongoing, historical reality. And in verse 32, in a most concise formula, he sums up the whole mystery of grace: God has imprisoned all people in disobedience in order to have compassion on all of them. The disobedience is not God's work, but the binding or jailing is. That's the second part of the hardening we studied.

"All people" refers to Gentiles and Jews. Neither has any ground to stand on or goodness to boast about before God. Both were imprisoned in disobedience. But God did this in order to show his mercy to all of them. "That is, on all without distinction rather than all without exception" (Bruce, *Romans*, p. 211). Then, when the "fullness of the Gentiles" and "all Israel" are saved by sheer grace and by such unimaginably just and compassionate ways, we can only stammer the doxology that Paul writes in verses 33-36.

To my mind, the close of the chapter clinches the argument for the view that the mystery consists of the wonderful ways in which God is gracious to Jews, then to Gentiles, and then again to Israel. These verses, especially verse 31, also show that "the salvation of all Israel" is not a matter of a future conversion miracle. Of course, God is free to cause any sudden mass conversion at any time. But when the question is asked whether verse 26 refers to a future conversion, the most likely interpretation is that Paul is speaking of an ongoing process in which Christians have been involved since the days of Paul himself.

So too the closing words about the "all" that were bound in disobedience so that God might have mercy on "all" help us to understand what Paul has been saying about the "full number of the Gentiles" and "all Israel." When, in verse

32, he can bundle together Jews and Gentiles as "all people" bound in disobedience and objects of mercy, he means to make no difference between the "full number of the Gentiles" in verses 12 and 25 and "all Israel" in verse 26. In both cases, the *fullness* refers to the totality of God's elect on the day of the Lord, representing "the Gentiles" on the one hand and "Israel" on the other.

The Church of Christ and the Future of Israel

Not everything Paul says in Romans 9 through 11 is clear to us. But we are clear about things Paul is *not* saying. He says nothing about a restored nation of Israel, or a return to land, or the rebuilding of a city. Nor does the rest of the New Testament.

Romans 11 *does* assure us that there is hope for disobedient Israel. God is not finished with this people. God made Israel the center of the world in the Old Testament. God saved a remnant in the New Testament. And God did not revoke his call of the rest, even if they are now jailed in disobedience.

We also do know from where the salvation of Israel is coming: from God, of course, through the channel of the church of Christ. And since the members of the church of Christ are overwhelmingly of Gentile origin, Israel's hope lies with the Gentiles. For just as the Gentiles received the gifts of God when Israel refused to accept, so Israel must now repossess its own inheritance, which has become the apostolic faith of a mostly Gentile church.

That's why it is so heartbreaking to think of the barriers the church has built between itself and the ethnic descendants of ancient Israel. How could we antagonize those whose bread we are eating! If we would only realize that we are living from someone else's wealth! If we would be clearly taught and made fully aware that the church is living in Israel's tents while most Israelites are still outside, then we would repent in sackcloth and ashes!

The Gentiles who have entered into the church of Christ and who have thereby received the citizenship papers of Israel (Eph. 2:11-18) must live so appealingly in the love of God that disobedient Israel becomes envious of our spiritual wealth (Rom. 10:19; 11:14). That can only happen when we have a deep knowledge of the grace of God, which gave us life. And when it happens, when God is so obviously present among us that even disobedient Israel wants to enter, the banquet hall will finally be filled. It will be the climax of the feast. "For if [Israel's] rejection is the reconciliation of the world, what will their acceptance be but life from the dead?" (Rom. 11:15).

One Lord, One People

In Romans 9-11 Paul contrasts Jews and Gentiles. He does not contrast Israel and the church. He considers himself and his Jewish fellow workers part of the church. And he certainly never teaches that God has different programs for the church of Christ and for Israel. On the contrary, even in this essay about the role of Israel in salvation history, he maintains that there is only one Lord and one people. "For there is no difference between Jew and Gentile—the same Lord is Lord of all and richly blesses all who call on him" (10:12).

Ethnic Israel is the original tree and the only tree. Gentiles who find the God of Israel through Jesus Christ "have been grafted in among the others and now share in the nourishing sap from the olive root" (11:17). There is one tree and not two. There is one people of God. A person either belongs to that people of God by God's grace—never by race—or does not belong to God's people at all.

It is wrong to teach that God has one ancient people that is now being regathered in Palestine, and that God has an additional New Testament people called the church of Christ. Such teaching takes away glory not only from the church, but also from Christ.

As for the political state of Israel, I do not believe that it has anything to do with the great Shepherd's gathering of his people. That state should be judged by the same standards of justice, fairness, and freedom by which all the other nations are judged. God *may* use its founding for a new overture in his redemptive activity. But we have not been told that God *will* do so.

However, the appearance of groups and congregations of Jews who believe and proclaim that Jesus is the Messiah *is* a sign of the coming kingdom. In 1996, Moishe Rosen of Jews for Jesus estimated that his group had some 50,000 members. This ought to warm the heart of all Christians.

Jews were first. Israel is God's oldest son. When a Jew becomes a Christian, he or she is *fulfilled.* But in a sense, Gentiles who become Christians must also become Jewish. Abraham becomes our pilgrim father. We must live by a collection of Jewish books called the Bible. And we worship a Jewish Messiah.

We must live and be the church in such a way that the oldest son will finally decide to come home to the feast that the father has prepared for the unworthy one, who was once lost but has now been found, who was once dead but is now alive.

Eternal Image (1998)

—Serguei Orgunov

CHAPTER 10

PROMISE AND FULFILLMENT:
THE INHERITANCE OF THE LAND

"The New is in the Old concealed, the Old is in the New revealed." With that little rhyme, originally from Augustine, generations have been taught the right relationship of the Old and the New Testaments, or Covenants. In the Old, God *said* it; in the new, God *did* it. The promise is in the Old Testament, the fulfillment is in the New; but there are still some promises outstanding.

The New is "concealed" in the Old Testament. Once we know the full revelation of the New, we see the same truth concealed in the Old. "The Old Testament in spiritualized form, that is, the Old Testament stripped of its temporal and sensuous form, is the New Testament" (Herman Bavinck, *The Last Things,* p. 96).

The Hebrews divided the Old Testament into three parts: Law, Prophets, and Writings. The Law and the Prophets are the most important. The expression "This is the Law and the Prophets" stands for "This is the teaching of the Old Testament." The golden rule—do to others what you would have them do to you—"sums up the Law and the Prophets" (Matt. 7:12). So does the basic law to love God above all and to love your neighbor as yourself (Matt. 22:37-40).

The books of Law, the five books of Moses, were, and still are, the heart and core of the religion of Judaism. In the Jewish way of reckoning, the books of the Prophets include those we call the Major Prophets (Isaiah, Jeremiah, and Ezekiel—but not Daniel!) and the Minor Prophets (Hosea till Malachi), which they called "The Book of the Twelve." The Prophets in the Jewish Bible also include Joshua, Judges, Samuel, and Kings. Their first recipients classified all the other books in the Old Testament as the Writings.

We will now look more specifically at prophecy. My first point is that "prophecy belief in modern American Culture," as Paul Boyer calls it, has a totally different flavor than the Hebrew understanding of prophecy. For one thing, modern prophecy pundits always start with the book of Daniel, which does not belong to the Prophets. Besides, we have been conditioned to think of the prediction of the future when we hear the word "prophecy." And such a mind-set can never understand why the Hebrews could place history writing from Judges to Kings under the heading of *prophecy.* Apparently, prophecy was a broad concept in the Old Testament.

Not a Mere Announcement

In North American Christian and evangelical circles, *prophecy* has come to mean *prediction*. The study of prophecy requires people skilled in solving prophetic puzzles. Prophecy conferences are sessions where teachers show how the prophetic jigsaw puzzle of the end time fits together.

J. Barton Payne, who wrote an *Encyclopedia of Biblical Prophecy,* prepared a multi-colored wall map called "The Prophecy Map of World History" (Harper & Row, 1974). It gives us "the 737 predictions of the Bible, listed by number, arranged according to their point of fulfillment." According to the map, history is the fulfillment of 737 predictions made by God. Every time a prediction is fulfilled, we can check it off and look for the next one.

People who view history as the fulfillment of a series of future events predicted by God through the prophets are usually fatalists:

- "War is coming and nobody can prevent it."

- "The Jewish temple is going to be rebuilt and nobody can stop it."

- "The land belongs to Israel because God has said it."

- "Russia will invade Israel because Ezekiel has predicted it."

- "A nuclear blast will blow away a third of mankind because it says so in the book of Revelation."

This view of prophecy as prediction does not do justice to the prophets and their message. The model for such fatalistic announcements of future events is not in the Bible but in astrology.

Prophetic Predictions in Context

What these American evangelicals call a prediction is often something else. For instance, the first of J. Barton Payne's 737 predictions is Genesis 2:17, "when you eat of [that tree] you will surely die." But the intent of these words of God is similar to the words of a mother who says, "If you touch that stove you're going to get burned." She does not intend to make a prediction, but to issue a warning. The purpose of her words is to keep her child away from the stove. God's purpose was to keep Adam and Eve from eating the fruit of the forbidden tree.

When the prophets made predictions of doom, they were not announcing an unavoidable fate. Prophetic predictions of judgment must be placed in a context of possible repentance and prayer on the part of people, and mercy on the part of God. When the prophet Isaiah said to Hezekiah, "This is what the Lord says: Put your house in order, because you are going to die" (2 Kings 20:1), God changed his mind in answer to the king's prayer and tears (vv. 2-6). The prophet Jonah announced to the big city: "Forty more days and Nineveh will

> "The conditional nature of prophecy, when taken seriously, raises serious questions about outlining what must or must not happen before the end. The study of biblical prophecy puts no one one-up on God, as if his every move were known beforehand. Because of human infidelity, some promises may have been nullified or amended. The prerogative to determine what lies ahead is always God's" (Joel B. Green, *How to Read Prophecy*, p. 103).

be overturned" (Jon. 3:4). But God had compassion on a hundred and twenty thousand people and "many cattle as well" (4:11) when the city repented. Jonah knew all along that Yahweh is "a God who relents from sending calamity" (4:2). And Jonah himself was neither the first, nor the last, to resent the fact that bad guys may escape just punishment and receive God's grace.

When prophets announce a future of hope or doom, their purpose is not to give a chart of future events. The purpose of such predictions is to make people walk with God in the present, inspired by hope, restrained by fear.

This is clearly stated in Jeremiah 18:

> 7If at any time I announce that a nation or kingdom is to be uprooted, torn down and destroyed, 8and if that nation I warned repents of its evil, then I will relent and not inflict on it the disaster I had planned. 9And if at another time I announce that a nation or kingdom is to be built up and planted, 10and if it does evil in my sight and does not obey me, then I will reconsider the good I had intended to do for it.
>
> —Jeremiah 18:7-10

When prophecy is reduced to prediction of a future fate, we get a picture that resembles Greek tragedy more than biblical prophecy. God's threats and promises are always made in the give-and-take of a covenant relationship.

Prediction and Fulfillment

Just as prophecy must not be reduced to the prediction of a future fate, so *fulfillment* is more than the execution of a predicted event. Yes, *fulfillment* is *also* the execution of a predicted event. For instance, a prediction by a prophet, or by Jesus, that a city will be destroyed is fulfilled when that city lies in ruins. But the New Testament idea of fulfillment is much more profound than what popular prophecy books make of it.

All premil prophecy preachers have a line that goes like this: "I believe that the prophecies about the last days will be literally fulfilled, just as the prophecies about Christ's first coming were literally fulfilled." That's how M. R. De Haan reasons (*Coming Events in Prophecy*, p. 15), as well as Hal Lindsey (*The Late Great Planet Earth*, p. 176) and John Hagee (*Beginning of the End*, p. 83).

This insistence on literal fulfillment and the claim that three hundred specific predictions were fulfilled in the first coming of Christ (Lindsey) are actually misleading. God's Messiah on the cross was a totally baffling fulfillment of the prophetic predictions and not something any literalist could have figured out.

We'll return to this matter of literalism in a little while. As for *fulfillment,* when the New Testament uses that expression, it means by it "to make full," "to fill up." Think of a container being filled with water. The "fullness of time" is the day when the barrel is full. You and I and all people are inclined to think that the flow of days and seasons and years and generations goes on forever and ever, but it isn't true. "When the time had fully come," when God's barrel was filled, so to speak, "God sent his Son, born of a woman, born under the law, to redeem those under law, that we might receive the full rights of sons" (Gal. 4:4). And when the time is "full" Christ will return.

When Jesus says about the Law and the Prophets, "I have not come to abolish them but to fulfill them" (Matt. 5:17), he means that he is going to teach the full meaning of Law and Prophets. Jesus is going to "fill them up." When we listen to Jesus' words and look at his life and death, we will fully know what God was saying to us in the Law and in the Prophets. We will learn what it means to love God above all and to love our neighbors as ourselves.

Moreover, when the New Testament writers declare that Jesus Christ fulfilled a certain Scripture, they are, more often than not, referring to a nonpredictive prophecy or psalm. Contrary to the position of the premils, who count them as literal fulfillments of prophetic predictions, the Old Testament did not *predict* that someone would betray the Messiah for thirty shekels of silver, that the Messiah's hands and feet would be pierced, that his garments would be divided by soldiers, that he would be forsaken by God, or that he would suffer thirst. And yet, though we cannot speak here of specific prediction, we confess with all Christians that when these things happened the Scriptures were fulfilled.

One cannot rightly say that David uttered a predictive prophecy when he complained, "Even my close friend, whom I trusted, he who shared my bread, has lifted up his heel against me" (Ps. 41:9). And it is odd to state that this prophecy was literally fulfilled in Judas's betrayal of Jesus (John 13:18). In fact, none of us would have thought of combining David's complaint and Judas's treachery if the New Testament had not taught us to read the Bible in this manner. But the relationship between the psalm and the Messiah is much stronger and much deeper than a prophetic prediction that gets a literal fulfillment. It reveals an identification of Jesus with the psalm-singer, especially the singer of the royal psalms. Jesus becomes the subject and the object of the songs. That is the *full-fillment.*

Jesus died with Psalm 22 in mind, so to speak: "My God, my God, why have you forsaken me? . . . All who see me mock me; they hurl insults, shaking their heads: 'He trusts in the LORD; let the LORD rescue him.' . . . My tongue sticks to the roof of my mouth; you lay me in the dust of death. . . . They have pierced my hands and my feet. . . . O my Strength, come quickly to help me" (Ps. 22:1, 7-8, 15-16, 19).

In a wondrous way, Christ filled up the suffering of the righteous who cry to God and cannot find him. In that sense the psalm was *fulfilled*. And the second half of Psalm 22 provides a thrilling vision of God's praise in "the congregation" (v. 22): an act of worship in which "all the ends of the earth" (v. 27) participate and "all the families of the nations" (v. 27) bow and acknowledge that "dominion belongs to the LORD" (v. 28). The psalm can be fully understood and meaningfully sung only by the New Testament church that has been brought to life by the death and resurrection of Jesus Christ.

The whole New Testament is the fulfillment of the whole Old Testament. The fulfillment does not only cover the realm of prophecy. The message and mission and incomplete covenant life of the Old find fulfillment in the New. This topic is too big for this book. But enough has been said, I hope, to show that a counting of "predictive prophecies" that have been "literally fulfilled"— Lindsey claims "more than 300," Hagee lists six—does not do justice to the biblical notion of fulfillment.

Why Jerusalem Killed the Prophets

Of course, God did reveal things to his prophets "in visions" and "in dreams" (Num. 12:6), things that ordinary people cannot see or know. One of the tests by which Israel would know if a prophet was a true or a false prophet was precisely the eventual fulfillment or nonfulfillment of what the prophet had predicted (Deut. 18:22). But another test was faithfulness to God's law (Deut. 13:1-5).

Prophecy is prediction and proclamation, with the emphasis on the latter. The prophets are God's P.A. system. Through them he addresses the world. In the New Testament, every Christian is a prophet. The visions and the dreams are for all who share the Spirit of God through Jesus Christ in these last days (Acts 2:17-18). Prophecy is the general gift of believers. Next to the general gift of knowing and proclaiming God's will, we still have the special gift of prophecy, which may include the knowledge of a future event: "[Agabus] stood up and through the Spirit predicted that a severe famine would spread over the entire Roman world" (Acts 11:28; see also 21:10).

The word of prophecy that God entrusts to all of us includes the knowledge of deeds God will do in the future. But it does not consist of fortune-telling.

Christian prophecy requires a fearless proclamation of God's will. A prophetic church insists on uprightness in a crooked world.

The prophets were not hated and killed because they predicted wondrous and terrible events in the distant future. The prophets in Israel were feared, respected, and hated because they exposed sin and hypocrisy and because they demanded faithful covenant living in the name of their Sender: "To the law and to the testimony! If they do not speak according to this word, they have no light of dawn" (Isa. 8:20). Jerusalem killed the prophets and stoned those who were sent to her (Matt. 23:37) because Jerusalem, like Cain, could not stand the words and actions of those who are righteous (see 1 John 3:12). The blood of the righteous cries to high heaven, from Abel to Zechariah, son of Berekiah (Matt. 23:35). This Zechariah was martyred in the dying days of the kingdom of Judah. "He stood before the people and said, 'This is what God says: "Why do you disobey the LORD's commands? You will not prosper. Because you have forsaken the LORD, he has forsaken you"'" (2 Chron. 24:20). Then "they stoned him to death in the courtyard of the LORD's temple" (v. 21).

Jesus mentions these two, Abel and Zechariah, because Abel is at the beginning of the Law (Gen. 4) and Zechariah is at the end of the Writings. Second Chronicles is the last book of the Hebrew Bible. So from the beginning to the end—we would say, from Genesis to Revelation—the blood of the righteous prophets was shed. And following the same pattern, Jerusalem would kill the righteous Prophet Jesus.

Prophets and prophetesses were, and should still be today, people who know, obey, and proclaim the word and will of God. It is necessary to stress this point in a time in which Christian magazines advertise fanciful schemes of future calamities mapped out by so-called "experts" in prophecy.

Promise, Fulfillment, and the Messiah

I must repeat that the main figure in the Book is the Messiah. The hope of all people of the Old Testament, from Adam to Malachi, was Jesus Christ. The fulfillment of all the promises of the Old Testament is ultimately Christ. "For no matter how many promises God has made, they are 'Yes' in Christ" (2 Cor. 1:20). What God said to our parents in paradise (Gen. 3:15), what he promised to Abraham and to David, what he pictured through Israel's service of sacrifice (see, for example, Lev. 16 concerning the day of atonement), and what he allowed the prophets to see from afar—all of them found fulfillment in Christ, or will be fulfilled in him. From the Old Testament we should be able to show that Christ is the fulfillment of the promises and predictions.

Jesus himself argued prophecy with his contemporaries: "How can the Son of David be the Lord of David?" (Matt. 22:41-46). And the book of Acts records that the apostles, when they spoke to the Jews, constantly argued from the Scriptures that Jesus was the Messiah. Yet the Bible also teaches explicitly that unless our eyes are opened by God the Father (Matt. 16:17) or by his Spirit, we do not know that Jesus is the Messiah.

Jesus is the fulfillment of the promises. But the Lord must open our eyes and he must open the (Old Testament) Scriptures—which is what he began to do after his resurrection: "And beginning with Moses and all the Prophets, he explained to them what was said in all the Scriptures concerning himself" (Luke 24:27). Verse 44 continues, "This is what I told you while I was still with you: Everything must be fulfilled that is written about me in the Law of Moses, the Prophets and the Psalms" (Luke 24:27, 44). In this last verse, Christ mentions the three divisions of the Hebrew Scriptures: Law, Prophets, and the Psalms as the book that heads the Writings.

It is not even enough that Christ opens the Scriptures for us, he must also open our hearts and minds: "Then he opened their minds so they could understand the Scriptures" (Luke 24:45).

Therefore a prayer for illumination is not a mere formality. Unless the Scriptures as well as our minds are opened by him who is the Word, the scrolls of the Law, the Prophets, and the Writings remain sealed. Therefore even diligent students of the ancient Hebrew Scriptures may still miss the key that unlocks their meaning. "You diligently study the Scriptures because you think that by them you possess eternal life. These are the Scriptures that testify about me, yet you refuse to come to me to have life" (John 5:39-40). Many Israelites still read the Old Covenant while "a veil covers their hearts" (2 Cor. 3:15), said Paul. And they will not see the glory that Moses saw on the mountain unless they turn to Christ (vv. 13-16).

The first sermon on the first Christian Pentecost (Acts 2) does not explain to us who the Holy Spirit is, but who *Jesus* is, because that's what the Holy Spirit came to do. The Spirit explains who Jesus is by having Peter quote from the prophet Joel and the book of Psalms. It is by the Word and the Spirit that people find Christ.

When apostles or evangelists present the Christian gospel, they quote the Old Testament to back up their message. But Christians read the old books differently than their Jewish listeners. The Spirit of God has *opened* the Scriptures to them. They know that the promises are fulfilled in Christ. The Psalms sing of Christ and Christ himself sings the Psalms. Light has fallen on the Books of the Old Covenant. In that light we see the light. Therefore we ought to read the Bible backward. We read the old in the light of the new. Of course, responsible interpreters begin by establishing the meaning of a passage by studying the words of the text and its setting within its context. We ask ourselves what the original message meant to its original hearers. But the message must also be placed in the context of the whole Bible. For it is in the light of the fulfillment, Jesus Christ, that the meaning of the books of the Old Covenant is clear.

The reasoning that begins with "predictive prophecy" and then speaks of "literal fulfillment" is, at best, simplifying the issue, and, at worst, misleading Bible readers. Even the prophets themselves did not know exactly what kind of salvation the Spirit of Christ was announcing through their mouths and pens. We who know Jesus Christ, his suffering and glory and the great salvation that is ours by faith in him, know what prophets were yearning to learn and angels were longing to see (1 Pet. 1:10-12).

Just as the Messiah was the main topic of Old Testament expectation, so Christ is the main topic of New Testament hope. We do not merely look for this or that event to happen. But we look for him!

A Misleading Claim

Dispensationalism's strong popular appeal for Bible-believing Christians rests in its claim that prophecy must be taken literally and that it will be literally fulfilled. Anything that God has said will happen just as he said it. "God says what he means and he means what he says." That phrase gets repeated very often. According to John F. Walvoord, prophetic Scriptures must be understood literally. That is the "normal and natural way" to interpret them, "except when a nonliteral interpretation is obviously indicated" (*Israel in Prophecy,* pp. 30, 51).

By their insistence on literal fulfillment, dispensationalists imply, and often spell out, that allegorical interpretation or spiritualizing is wrong and is a sign of unbelief. I will show later on that the New Testament often does what they call "spiritualizing."

Two things must be said at this point. First, nobody, but nobody, gives a consistently literal interpretation of prophecy. Hal Lindsey, who is probably the loudest in proclaiming literal interpretation as the "golden rule" (*The Late Great Planet Earth,* p. 50), does not stick to it. When the Bible says that Christ will return on the clouds of heaven, Lindsey chooses to "believe that the clouds refer to the myriads of believers who return in white robes with Jesus" (p. 173). But a lake of blood in the Valley of Megiddo as deep as the horses' bridles and two hundred miles long *must* be taken literally (pp. 165-166). Though none hold to literalism consistently, all dispensational premils believe that Abraham's literal, fleshly descendants will inherit literal real estate—a claim I will come back to later.

Second, we should not forget why dispensational premils are so insistent on literal fulfillment and on the "normal and natural way to interpret prophecy," as John F. Walvoord would have it. They want to safeguard the Bible's accessibility to lay people by sticking to the plain meaning of the text. They are suspicious of church tradition (such as formulated by Augustine). And they used to be leery of biblical scholarship. They regard allegorical or spiritual explanations of difficult texts and hard-to-believe predictions as a cover-up for unbelief. Therefore they quote the Bible and affirm, "God says what he means and he means what he says." (In order to learn how to dialogue with these fellow Christians see Vern S. Poythress, *Understanding Dispensationalists.*) Although some of their slogans may be repeated for rhetorical effect—liberals aren't the only ones who know what their audience wants to hear—I share their desire to assure God's church of the reliability of God and of God's Word. And I believe that the good world that God promised is coming, literally, when he makes a new earth. But we must also instruct God's church to let the New Testament decide how Old Testament promises are fulfilled.

The Promised Land in the Old Testament

In the Old Testament, the Promised Land is at the heart of the covenant with Abraham and his seed. All the promised blessings of God would be enjoyed in the land, which is the tangible inheritance of God's people. The writers of the Old Testament believed that God faithfully fulfilled these promises to Abraham, including the promise of the land. God said that Abraham's children would be as numerous as "dust of the earth" and "stars in the sky" (Gen. 13:16; 15:5). Moses considered this promise fulfilled: "today you are as many as the stars in the sky" (Deut. 1:10). Of course, these expressions are typical figures of speech and grand exaggerations. We should not take them literally. Nobody can count the sand at the seashore, the dust of the earth, or the stars in the sky. But the point is that hundreds of thousands came from a woman who was barren and a man "as good as dead" because God made the promise and Abraham believed (Heb. 11:11-12).

After the conquest of the promised land, the writer of the book of Joshua said, "Not one of all the LORD's good promises to the house of Israel failed; every one was fulfilled" (Josh. 21:45). One might say that the land was not as big as the LORD had promised it would be. God had said he gave them the land "from the river of Egypt to the great river, the Euphrates" (Gen. 15:18; Ex. 23:31). Later, however, the writer of the book of Kings considered this promise fulfilled during the reign of Solomon (1 Kings 4:21).

Israel lost the land through their disobedience. They were displaced and scattered to the countries of their enemies. But the prophets, even those who explained contemporary happenings as the judgment of God, also promised a regathering of the people and a return to the land. This return took place under the leadership of Ezra, Nehemiah, Zerubbabel, the son of David, and Joshua the high priest. However, the land was never fully free after the exile. "We are slaves in the land you gave us," said Nehemiah in his prayer of confession (Neh. 9:36). Except for a short period under the Maccabees, the people of Israel were under foreign rulers in their own land until A.D. 70, and then they lost the land, the capital city, and their temple.

The Promised Land in the New Testament

In chapter 7 we saw how Abraham became the father of many nations and had more children, in Christ, than any Old Testament believer could have imagined. All believers incorporated in Christ, regardless of race, enjoy the covenant blessings of their father Abraham. So what happened to the promise of the land? Our premil friends believe that the promise still stands, and that it is reserved for the biological descendants of Abraham. However, if we accept the teaching of the New Testament as the norm for the understanding of the Old Testament, the promise of land was an Old Testament symbol of an inheritance that is vastly bigger than the piece of real estate bordering the Mediterranean Sea. In the New Testament, the inheritance of God's children is God himself, as well as the whole renewed universe.

This reinterpretation of the land is clearest in the epistle to the Hebrews. The promised land, where God's people find rest at last, can be entered only by faith in God. In the past, many could not enter because of their unbelief. They sinned and their bodies fell in the desert. As for us, the promised land still lies ahead. "Today, if you hear his voice, do not harden your hearts" (Heb. 3:7). Trust and obey. Follow the better Joshua, who leads us to rest in the promised land (3:7-4:11).

All believers from both the Old and New Covenants are pilgrims. They have no country in which they are truly at home. With Abraham, who modeled our faith and hope, all believers look "forward to the city with foundations, whose architect and builder is God" (11:10).

A similar teaching that God's people are strangers here below, exiles looking for the homeland, pervades 1 Peter (1:1; 2:11). God's people, saved by Christ, bear the titles of Old Covenant Israel: "a chosen people, a royal priesthood, a holy nation" (2:9, see also Ex. 19:6). But their inheritance is not the passing beauty of the good land to which Israel traveled under the leadership of Moses (see, for example, Deut. 8). By a new birth they have come "into an inheritance that can never perish, spoil or fade—kept in heaven for you" (1 Pet. 1:4). The text does not say that the inheritance is heaven, but that it is guarded by God in heaven; which means that it is everlastingly safe. And since the inheritance is undefiled, imperishable, and unfading, it is of a different order than anything and everything we know in our present form of existence.

For Paul all the Old Testament promises are fulfilled, or will be completely fulfilled, in Christ. That also holds for the promise of the land. At first glance he does not seem to speak of the land because neither the gospel nor God's people are any longer tied to a particular territory or a particular nation. But a careful look shows that the apostle reinterprets the Old Testament promise of Canaan into a New Testament promise of a new world! See how he restates the fifth commandment: The Old Covenant law said, "Honor your father and your mother so that you may live long in the land the LORD your God is giving you" (Ex. 20:12; Deut. 5:16). That land was Canaan, to which Israel was traveling. But Paul says in Ephesians 6:2-3, "'Honor your father and mother'—which is the first commandment with a promise—'that it may go well with you and that you may enjoy long life on the earth.'" The promise is still valid, but the territory is enlarged to encompass "the earth"!

Notice also how Paul sums up the promises to Abraham and his descendants in Romans 4:13. Paul reinterprets the promise that the descendants of Abraham would inherit the land of Canaan by saying that "Abraham and his offspring received the promise that he would be heir of the world." The inheritance is not merely the land of Palestine but the cosmos. Abraham and his offspring inherit the world. And since we, who believe and belong to Christ, are Abraham's offspring and heirs (Gal. 3:29), we are heirs of that world. In Christ the whole world is ours already (1 Cor. 3:21). But Paul is thinking of the new world for which all of creation and we ourselves are now groaning, hoping, and praying (Rom. 8:18-27). And just like Peter, Paul teaches that this inheritance will be imperishable and immortal, for it is the kingdom of God that the saints will inherit (1 Cor. 15:50-57).

This shift, or, should we say, this enlargement of the inheritance from the land of Canaan to "the earth" or "the kingdom," is found in the preaching of Jesus himself. When he speaks of the inheritance that is due to the "blessed" of God, Jesus names it "the earth" or "the kingdom of heaven" (Matt. 5:3-10; 25:34).

In the New Testament, the promise of the land as the inheritance of God's people is neither cancelled nor postponed, but fulfilled. The inheritance is not spiritualized in the New Testament, as some say. (And when they say it, they mean that the Old Testament inheritance is the real thing.) But in the New Testament the inheritance is enlarged and enriched. God promised silver but he gives us gold. The better Joshua is leading us to the land that flows with milk and honey where we must sing the song of Moses and the Lamb (Deut. 31:19-20; Rev. 15:3-4): "Great and marvelous are your deeds, Lord God Almighty."

The Old is in the New fulfilled. It's not cancelled but made full and mature. The inheritance is now ours by faith. We have the firstfruits of the Spirit, which is our foretaste of the new country—just as the Israelites received a cluster of grapes from the Valley of Eshcol in the promised land (Rom. 8:23; Num. 13:23). The land, the real land, the whole earth, will be ours when our last enemy is destroyed (1 Cor. 15:26). And all that has life will praise the Lord.

The Last Judgment, detail

—Fra Angelico, c. 1400-1455

CHAPTER 11

PROMISE AND FULFILLMENT:
THE CITY AND THE TEMPLE

When the New Testament determines our understanding of God's promises in the Old, we see

- *the land* promised to Abraham as a pledge of the real country of God's people

- *the city* of Jerusalem in Palestine as a symbol of the real city where God will dwell with us

- *the temple* in Jerusalem as God's promise of the eventual temple in which God shall be all in all

Jerusalem, O, Jerusalem

Since the times of David and Solomon, the religion of Israel was centered around Jerusalem because God lived there. God lived in that city in a more literal sense than we are inclined to believe. This was his address on earth. Therefore God's people knew no greater joy than to go up to Jerusalem. They had a special section in their songbook that they sang when they were "going up" to Jerusalem—Psalms 120 to 134, the songs of ascents. The Israelites seemingly pictured God more often in Jerusalem than in heaven (Ps. 87:1; 99:1; 100). The exiles look to Jerusalem as their real home (Ps. 42:4; 43:4; 84; and others). Daniel does not look to heaven, but toward Jerusalem, when he prays to God three times a day (Dan. 6:10). The Israelites knew no greater joy than to be in Jerusalem and no greater sadness than to see this city destroyed (Ps. 137; see also Ps. 126).

For the prophets the terms *Jerusalem* and *daughter of Jerusalem* are shorthand for the people of God. God's blessings are upon this city when Israel prospers. But when Jerusalem lies in ruins, "the Lord has covered the Daughter of Zion with the cloud of his anger" (Lam. 2:1). The New Testament follows this particular way of speaking. Therefore the writings of the New Testament say little or nothing about the promises of the land, but much about the lot of Jerusalem.

Jerusalem rejects the prophets and crucifies Jesus. Jesus weeps over the city (Luke 19:41) and predicts its end (Matt. 24; Mark 13; Luke 23). The leaders of the people are responsible for the rejection of Jesus. But God has chosen the rejected stone (Jesus) as the capstone for the new building (Matt. 21:42, among others). Jesus tells the Jewish leaders, "The kingdom of God will be taken away from you and given to a people who will produce its fruit" (Matt. 21:43).

The final confrontation between Jesus and the Jewish leaders and the subsequent death and resurrection of the Messiah mark the end of Jerusalem as the city where God dwells. From now on, Jerusalem is not the holy city and the land of Israel is no longer the holy land. But these events do not mark the end of God's mercy for the people of Israel, as we have seen in chapter 9.

Where Is God's Jerusalem?

In a very remarkable parable (Gal. 4:21-31), Paul compares the earthly Jerusalem of his days with the heavenly city of his faith. The earthly Jerusalem, the heart of Judaism, claims to be Abraham's offspring. Yes, Paul agrees, these Judaists who live by the law and not by faith are children of Abraham. But he reminds the Galatians that Abraham had two sons, one born according to the flesh (Ishmael, the son of Abraham and Hagar) and the other brought forth by the power of the promise (Isaac, the son of Abraham and Sarah). "The present city of Jerusalem" (v. 25) is the child of Hagar and all she represents: slavery, law-keeping, the Sinai covenant. The present Jerusalem does not represent new covenant but old covenant, not faith in the promise but works of the law, not freedom in the Spirit but bondage in the flesh. However, the children of Sarah are free. And Sarah is represented by the "Jerusalem that is above" (v. 26). The citizens of that city live by faith. They have been generated by the promise and they have escaped the condemnation of the law.

This parable is enormously instructive. First, it shows that for Paul the historical city of Jerusalem had lost its significance as the holy city whose citizens are God's beloved children. If today's Christians would allow this word to sink into their consciousness, they would cease their endless territorial discussions about Jerusalem and, perhaps, their pilgrimages to that city.

Second, this story in Galatians 4 shows that Paul thinks of the new Jerusalem as a present reality. One belongs either to the earthly or to the heavenly city. Note how Paul compares the two. He calls the first one "the present city of Jerusalem" (v. 25). But he does not contrast it with the future city of Jerusalem. Instead he contrasts it with a city that is also a present reality. However, that city is not below but it is above. Why is it above? Because that's where Jesus is. In a similar vein he speaks of our "citizenship" being in heaven, from where we expect our Savior to come (Phil. 3:20).

Third, this parable shows us that the Old Testament promises concerning the future glory of Jerusalem apply to "the Jerusalem that is above" and not to the city in Palestine. Paul writes, "The Jerusalem that is above is free, and she is our mother. For it is written: 'Be glad, O barren woman, who bears no children; break forth and cry aloud, you who have no labor pains; because more are the children of the desolate woman than of her who has a husband'" (Gal. 4:26-27).

Isaiah 54:1, the original prophecy from which Paul quotes, shows how great and glorious Zion will be after the exile in Babylon. Isaiah promises that the daughter of Zion, who at the time of the exile was like a forsaken woman, will later have more children than she had before the time of her rejection. Paul sees the fulfillment of that promise in the gathering of the believers in Christ—not only Jewish, but also Gentile believers. That's why the daughter of Zion has so many children.

This is a very compact and very revealing statement. The barren Sarah brought forth a son by the power of the Word of promise (Isaac). Sarah's children (the children of the new Jerusalem) are the children of the promise. They are all brought forth by the gospel of Jesus Christ. In this way the barren woman, Israel, becomes the mother of many, and the glory of Zion becomes greater than ever. It happens by the divine Word of power by which Jews and Gentiles receive life and are counted as the heirs of the promise made to Abraham (Gal. 3:29).

Jerusalem in Hebrews

All the Old Testament predictions about the future glory of Jerusalem have been fulfilled, or are being fulfilled. But the New Testament locates Jerusalem, where Jesus is, above, in heaven. This is also the case in the epistle to the Hebrews. The old temple, the old country, and the old Jerusalem are all part of the Old Covenant. And the Old remains incomplete, fruitless, and unfulfilled without the New (see 11:40 for just one example). The earthly, old Jerusalem does not embody the hope. The hope is in a better country (11:16) and a new city. That's where we are going, and, we may also say, that's where we already are. For just as Paul spoke of the existence of the heavenly Jerusalem and our citizenship in it as a present reality—though not yet visible—so does Hebrews. "You have come to Mount Zion, to the heavenly Jerusalem, the city of the living God" (12:22). You *have come*, it says. That means you are there now.

In the epistle to the Hebrews, all provisions of the old Sinai covenant are temporary. They are mere symbols of the coming reality of the New Covenant. But we have now reached the realities that Moses saw on the mountain of which the earthly was a copy and shadow (8:5). Now the shadows are past and the real thing is here (9:24; 10:1).

The basic assumption of dispensationalism that the earthly is real and the heavenly is "only" spiritual is squarely opposed to the teaching of Hebrews. The heavenly is the real thing, of which the earthly is only sign and symbol. And so it is with the earthly and the heavenly Jerusalem. The old has had its time, just as the sanctuary that was in it. Jesus had no place in old Jerusalem. He suffered outside the city gate (13:12). The Jewish Christians who read this letter should also give up on the old city and bear disgrace with Jesus. "For here we do not have an enduring city, but we are looking for the city that is to come" (13:14).

It is coming and it is a present reality. In our worship we are already united on Mount Zion in the heavenly Jerusalem with the joyful angels, the righteous who went before us, with God the Judge, and Jesus the Mediator of a New Covenant (12:22-24). We belong already to that city because our names are written there.

Psalm 87 and the New Jerusalem

The Old Testament promises of the future glory of Jerusalem become reality in the New Testament city of God. According to the traditional interpretation, Psalm 87 is the only psalm, though certainly not the only passage, that foresees a city that counts Israel's former enemies among its citizens. God gives them the birthright and citizenship of those born within the walls of Zion. "As they make music they will sing, 'All my fountains are in you'" (Ps. 87:7).

This vision becomes reality in the New Testament. Also in the book of Revelation the new, or heavenly, Jerusalem—"the city of my God" (Rev. 3:12), where the faithful members of Christ's church are registered—is contrasted with another city, a great and worldly city. This latter city is sometimes called Babylon, sometimes Rome. But it is also the city where the "Lord was crucified" (11:8), that is, Jerusalem (see also 17:18). Just as those "who claim to be Jews though they are not, but are liars" (3:9) are contrasted with the true Israel, "those who obey God's commandments and hold to the testimony of Jesus" (12:17), so there appears to be a contrast between the two cities of Jerusalem. The new, heavenly Jerusalem is God's own "construction." It is also the bride of Christ (21:2, 9), which is the church of Christ (2 Cor. 11:2; Eph. 5:32).

As we have seen, the daughter of Jerusalem, or Jerusalem itself, is shorthand throughout the Bible for the people of God as well as for their inheritance. And so it is in the closing chapters of the Bible.

The Temple

The heart of Israel was Jerusalem and the heart of Jerusalem was the temple. For a thousand years before the birth of Christ, the holiest place on earth was the inner sanctum of the temple on Mount Zion. God was there—not visibly, for human eyes cannot see the God of Israel. And God was not "contained" in the temple. "The heavens, even the highest heaven, cannot contain you. How much less this temple I have built!" said Solomon in his prayer of dedication (1 Kings 8:27). But God did really live there.

However, Jesus terminated the religious significance of the temple as the place of atonement when he, as the Lamb of God, brought the last sacrifice for sin on the last altar, which was Golgotha. When he cried "Finished!" he ended the seemingly endless row of bloody sacrifices, as well as the Aaronic priesthood that made these offerings. Never again do we need another sacrifice for our sins. We have everlasting peace with God "through the sacrifice of the body of Jesus Christ once for all" (Heb. 10:10).

God underlined the significance of Christ's atoning sacrifice for the temple service: "The curtain of the temple was torn in two from top to bottom" (Matt. 27:51). Now "we have confidence to enter the Most Holy Place by the blood of Jesus" (Heb. 10:19). All of us may go directly to God our Father, and none of us is any longer dependent on a human mediator. Young and old, male and female, Jew and Gentile, may go to God "in full assurance of faith" (10:22) because Jesus has opened the way to the Father.

Jesus is the fulfillment of the temple. He is "greater than the temple" (Matt. 12:6). And he makes the Jerusalem temple superfluous. In the new era, marked by the coming and work of Christ, it no longer matters where God is worshiped, only how. "Worshipers must worship in spirit and in truth" (John 4:24).

Especially the gospel according to John presents Jesus as the temple. The temple was the place where the glory of God resided. But now, in the human Jesus, the glory of God has "tabernacled among us" (1:14—from the Greek). The temple was the place where the sins of people were atoned for. But now John points to Jesus: "Look, the Lamb of God, who takes away the sin of the world!" (1:29). "Jesus is both the place of atonement and the place of God's presence" (David E. Holwerda, *Jesus and Israel*, p. 75).

John also identifies Christ as the temple of God, from whom water flows that brings life to a dying world, as prophesied in Zechariah 14:8 and Ezekiel 47. Jesus taught this especially on the climactic day of the Feast of Tabernacles, when he called all thirsty ones to come to him and drink. The life-giving water by which Christ brings healing and refreshment is the Holy Spirit (John 7:37-39).

In the New Testament epistles, the Christian community is the temple (1 Cor. 3:16; 2 Cor. 6:16; Eph. 2:21; 1 Pet. 2:5). Of course there is no contradiction between them and the gospels. In John 17 Jesus says that he had entrusted the glory of the Father to his disciples and that, as the Father dwells in the Son, so the Son will dwell in the church (vv. 20-23). The church is now God's address on earth.

God's presence in the church becomes clear after Pentecost. It is the general teaching of the New Testament that between Christ's ascension and return God is present on earth by the Holy Spirit. And the people of God form the temple, the dwelling place of God.

Throughout its history the church of Christ is tempted to designate a holy building as God's dwelling place on earth. But Christians themselves are God's holy building, not the place where they meet for worship. Christians don't go *to* the temple, they *are* God's temple. Never again does God live in a building of wood and stone.

Paul emphasizes this in 1 Corinthians 3:16: "You yourselves are God's temple." The *you* in this verse is plural. Of course, if God lives in all of us, then he dwells in each of us. In chapter 6 of the same letter he asks, "Do you not know that your body is a temple of the Holy Spirit, who is in you, whom you have received from God? You are not your own . . . " (v. 19). Although the *your* and the *you*s in these sentences are still plural, Paul obviously addresses his warning against sexual immorality to each person. Yet the New Testament never speaks of Christians as a bunch of temples. Together we are the sacred temple of God (see 1 Cor. 3:17).

We misunderstand God's salvation history when we think that the real temple existed in the Old Testament and that the Christian church only *resembles* the temple or is an allegorical temple. It's the other way around. God's promise to dwell among his people has a history of fulfillment. In Leviticus 26:11-12 God promised, "I will put my dwelling place among you, and I will not abhor you. I will walk among you and be your God, and you will be my people." The tabernacle, and later the temple, were an initial fulfillment of this promise. But they were merely a symbol and prelude of the real manifestation of God in his New Testament church. Now God has come to be among us, not to dwell behind a curtain in a forbidding building. God has invaded our very lives with his holiness. "For we are the temple of the living God" (2 Cor. 6:16). Now the word of Leviticus is fulfilled: "I will live with them and walk among them, and I will be their God, and they will be my people" (2 Cor. 6:16).

God is not only *among* us, so that we can point to a tent or a temple, but God is *in* us. We are not only his people, but we are his "sons and daughters" (2 Cor. 6:18). The fulfillment of the promise of God's nearness as our covenant God is like filling up a cup; it's ever fuller. The holiness of the Spirit-filled church of the New Testament is much more awesome than the holiness of Israel because it is more intense and internal.

Still, we look forward to the day when the cup will be full and running over. When God and we shall dwell together on the new earth, in the new Jerusalem, the ancient promise will be full: "Now the dwelling ("tent" or "tabernacle") of God is with men and he will live ("tabernacle") with them. They will be his people and God himself will be with them and be their God" (Rev. 21:3). These are the stages of fulfillment: a portable tabernacle, a permanent building, a dedicated people of God, a sin-free togetherness in the new world. And there's no turning back.

The Ezekiel Temple

Dispensationalists believe that the ideal temple described in the visions of Ezekiel (40-47:12) will be operational in Jerusalem during the time when Jesus sits there on the throne, that is, during the millennium.

Ezekiel was a priest who belonged to the early group of deported exiles in Babylon. There God called him to be a prophet. To his fellow Jews Ezekiel announced the terror-filled judgments of God that climaxed in the desecration of the temple and the burning of Jerusalem on the day his wife died (ch. 24).

His vision of the beautiful temple was the climactic finish of his work as a prophet. The vision declares that, in the end, all things will be good again: the temple will be more beautiful than ever before, the priests will be truly holy. The

According to the schedule of future events in premil books, the Israeli people must rebuild a temple in Jerusalem before the Antichrist comes, and the Antichrist must desecrate it during "the tribulation." Then, after the seven-year period, Christ will come for the millennial reign and the "Ezekiel temple" must be built. For a thousand years, this Ezekiel temple will be earth's center of worship.

The *New Scofield Study Bible* rejects a symbolic interpretation—it claims that the temple will be erected according to Ezekiel's blueprint "subsequent to Israel's regathering and conversion" and "in keeping with God's prophetic program for the millennium." Nearly all dispensationalists follow Scofield's note.

But the literal interpretation runs into great difficulties explaining the rules on the sacrificial service in this ideal temple. These sacrifices are sin offerings (43:19f.) offered to God for atonement; they expiate sins (45:15, 17, 20). In this instance, however, the Scofield Bible doesn't take the text literally. The footnote for 43:19 argues that the sacrificial service must be understood either as a memorial service, reminding Israel of Christ's once-for-all atoning sacrifice, or "the reference to sacrifices is not to be taken literally . . . but is rather to be regarded as a presentation of the worship of redeemed Israel in her own land in the millennial temple, using the terms with which the Jews were familiar in Ezekiel's day."

A. A. Hoekema rightly calls this footnote "a far-reaching concession on the part of dispensationalists. If the sacrifices are not to be taken literally, why should we take the temple literally?" (*The Bible and the Future,* p. 204). Dispensational Christians realize that sacrificial rites in Ezekiel's temple are not permissible after the death and resurrection of Jesus. But there is much more they should protest: the holy place of wood and stone is outdated. The holy priesthood that mediates for ordinary people is no longer fitting. Neither is the whole concept of ritual holiness. The regulation prohibiting the uncircumcised and foreigners from approaching the sanctuary disregards the work of Christ Jesus. The localized presence of God portrayed by Ezekiel would be inconsistent after Pentecost. And so on.

The idea of a literal millennial temple according to the blueprint of Ezekiel (but with memorial sacrifices!) is certainly one of the weakest links in the whole dispensational system.

glory of God himself will once again return to the holy house (44:4-8) and the people will redivide the land (47:14-48:35).

So Ezekiel announced a future of restoration and forgiveness in words that were understandable to the exiles he was sent to comfort. The New Testament shows how Israel's hope was fulfilled in and by the Messiah. Christ is the fulfillment of Ezekiel's temple. In him the glory of the LORD has returned and will return (Ezek. 43; John 1:14; 2 Cor. 3:18; Col. 3:4).

By his atoning death, Jesus fulfilled the temple service. Christ has opened the sanctuary of God (the torn curtain), not to desecrate it, but to permit the holiness of God to flow into the secular world—an ever-deeper stream of healing water, which is the Spirit of God (Ezek. 47). This is the saving work of Jesus, which has been going on since his resurrection (John 7:37-39). And the final fulfillment is the new City.

When John pictures it, he uses features borrowed from Ezekiel's temple. There are general features, such as the measurements and symmetry and the glitter of the glory of the Lord, but also particulars, such as the names of the twelve tribes on the twelve gates (Rev. 21:12-13) and the river from the throne of God that brings healing and life (22:1-2). These come from Ezekiel (48:30f.; 47:1, 14) and from Zechariah (14:8).

At the same time, Revelation 21 and 22 point us to an even further fulfillment: the New Jerusalem has all the holiness and wholeness and glory of Ezekiel's temple, but it is a *city*. "I did not see a temple in the city, because the Lord God Almighty and the Lamb are its temple" (Rev. 21:22). All of the city is temple, because God is all in all. That's the goal of life and of God's salvation history. We long for the fulfillment.

Gathering and Building

In general the Old Testament prophets announce the great future in terms that are familiar to their hearers. Jerusalem will be rebuilt, the exiles will be regathered, the temple service will be reinstituted, and the promised land will be more prosperous than ever. We should admit that we do the same thing when we attempt to form an image of the world to come. (That's why people always ask if they will recognize their loved ones in heaven.) And we should also note that the prophets frequently transcend the earthly and national conditions when they say the future kingdom will encompass the whole world (see, for example, Ps. 72) and will consist of a recreation of heaven and earth (Isa. 60:19-20; 65:17).

What the prophets intended to say, or what the Spirit of Christ who was in them (1 Pet. 1:11) was actually pointing to, is determined by the New

Testament. And the New Testament declares that the Lord returned to Zion when Jesus was born in Bethlehem.

> Burst into songs of joy together, you ruins of Jerusalem,
> for the LORD has comforted his people,
> he has redeemed Jerusalem.
>
> —Isaiah 52:9

Simeon, who waited all of his life for the "consolation of Israel" (Luke 2:25) now asks to be dismissed from his watch, "For my eyes have seen your salvation" (v. 30). And the prophetess Anna belonged to a group of people "who were looking forward to the redemption of Jerusalem" (Luke 2:38). Now they see the Redeemer. The consolation of Israel and the redemption of Jerusalem have begun because the Messiah is here.

And how is Jerusalem rebuilt by the Messiah? That is the story of Christ's death and resurrection, ascension, outpouring of the Spirit, sending of the apostles, and the building of the church that is still going on today. Jesus said, "I will build my church" (Matt. 16:18).

Whenever the words *building, to build,* and *builder* are used in the New Testament in connection with the church, they never refer to a building of wood and stone, but always to people. The building imagery is plentiful. Jesus calls himself a builder (Matt. 16:18), but more often a stone (Matt. 21:42). He is the *foundation* on which all of us must be built (1 Cor. 3:11). We might also call him *the chief cornerstone* (Eph. 2:20) that holds the whole building together (2:21).

The original "apostles and prophets" might also be called the *foundation,* because their testimony concerning Jesus Christ constitutes the basis of the church. Everyone who is interested in "the redemption of Jerusalem" can see the building program. We see "the holy temple" rising (2:21). Everyone must come to *the Stone* (1 Pet. 2:4-8) and become attached to him as *living stones.* Then we can offer the spiritual sacrifices in Zion's temple (1 Pet. 2:5-6), which are the fulfillment of the old temple service. The old was only a shadow of the things that have now come; "the reality, however, is found in Christ" (Col. 2:17).

That's how the New reveals the meaning of the Old. "The spiritualization of the Old Testament, rightly understood, is not an invention of Christian theology but has its beginning in the New Testament itself. The Old Testament in spiritualized form, that is, the Old Testament stripped of its temporal and sensuous form, is the New Testament" (Herman Bavinck, *The Last Things,* p. 96).

The gathering of God's people by the Messiah through his Word and Spirit *is* the fulfillment of the promised gathering of Israel. The building up of the corporate house, the body of Christ, the spiritual temple, *is* the reconstruction of Jerusalem.

The Restoration of David's House

When the Gentiles began to accept the gospel of Jesus Christ, the question arose of whether or not they should be circumcised and taught to keep the law of Moses. Notice that such a question could arise only because the converted Gentiles were now regarded as part of the restored Israel. They shared in all the privileges of God's people and the question was whether or not, just as all Christian Jews, they should also submit to the obligations—"be circumcised and required to obey the law of Moses" (Acts 15:5).

As in all assemblies of the church, there was a left and a right, a liberal and a conservative element in the meeting. Paul and Barnabas preached the gospel of "nothing but the cross of Jesus" and some would have considered them "liberal." Way at the other end of the spectrum were those believers in Christ who belonged to the party of the Pharisees (v. 5). Simon Peter must have surprised the group when he solidly backed Paul (vv. 7-11). The chairman, James, the brother of Jesus—comparing Matthew 13:55 and Galatians 2:9 makes me assume he was the chairman—was a thoroughly Jewish, conservative Christian. Notice how he calls Peter *Simeon* (Acts 15:14). And see the epistle of James, which he addressed to "the twelve tribes in the *diaspora*" (James 1:1—from the Greek). James made a speech of his own (Acts 15:13-21) in which he first quoted Scripture to show that what was going on was God's work in accordance with God's Word. Then he proposed the content of a letter to be sent to the Christians of the Gentiles. This proposal was accepted by the assembly.

> [14]"Simeon has related how God first looked favorably on the Gentiles, to take from among them a people for his name. [15]This agrees with the words of the prophets, as it is written, [16]'After this I will return and I will rebuild the dwelling of David, which has fallen; from its ruins I will rebuild it, and I will set it up, [17]so that all other peoples may seek the Lord—even all the Gentiles over whom my name has been called. Thus says the Lord, who has been making these things [18]known from long ago.'"
>
> —Acts 15:14-18, NRSV

James says that the words of the prophets (plural in v. 15) are in agreement with Simon Peter's claim that God is now calling a people for himself from among the Gentile nations. Also, at the end, he says that God "has been making these things known from long ago" (vv. 17-18, NRSV). Therefore, although he is going to quote only the prophet Amos, James concedes that what Peter has reported is in line with the ancient prophetic Word.

What, then, had God promised? That he would *re*visit his people, *re*build David's dwelling, and *re*build and *re*structure the ruins. (Note the four words that promise renewal of God's care for his people.)

Then the prophecy James quotes turns to the people who are not connected with the dwelling of David. They are called "all other peoples" (v. 17, NRSV) or "the remnant of men" (NIV) or "the rest of mankind" (NKJV). The parallel line, "all the Gentiles," shows who are meant. Not all Gentiles, but "those over whom my name has been called" (v. 17, NRSV). Those are the ones who have learned the name of their Savior God. Compare this with Isaiah 44:5: "One will say, 'I belong to the LORD'; another will call himself by the name of Jacob; still another will write on his hand, 'The LORD's,' and will take the name Israel."

The prophecy James quotes from Amos 9:11-12 has some problems. But the role of the quotation in the speech of James is quite clear. The reestablishment of the house of David and the ingathering of the Gentiles coincide. They take place now that Jesus is Lord and the gospel of forgiveness and renewal is being proclaimed. Here the New Testament shows how God renews the glory of David's house as he promised in the Old Testament.

Acts 15:16-18 does not quote Amos 9:11-12 from the Hebrew text but from the early Greek translation called the *Septuagint* (abbreviated *LXX*). In the Hebrew and our English translation of Amos 9:12, the result of the restoration of David's house is "that they may possess the remnant of Edom." That refers to the land of the enemy. In the LXX "they will possess" became "they will seek" and "the rest of Edom" became "the rest of *Adam*" (that is, *mankind*). James quoted the LXX because it said what he wanted to say.

According to the dispensationalists, James is outlining God's plan for the last days along the lines of Darby and Scofield:

First comes the "church-age," limited to verse 14. "After this I will return" refers to Christ's second coming, they say. At the second coming Christ will reestablish the throne of David for a thousand years and restore Israel as a nation (v. 16). The "remnant of mankind" of verse 17 are the Jews who, with the Gentiles who are incorporated into Israel, enter into the millennial reign of Christ.

However, this interpretation is very unnatural. It makes James suddenly speak about a millennium far beyond the horizon, instead of about the matter at hand. Besides, the future tense ("After this I will return . . . I will rebuild . . . ") belongs to the prophecy of Amos. And to divide verse 17 into two groups, Jews and Gentiles, runs counter to normal reading.

The point of James is that the prophecy of Amos is being fulfilled *now*.

The Seventh Angel with an Open Book, from Apocalypse   —Giusto di Giovanni Menabuoi, 1363-1393

CHAPTER 12

WHAT WE EXPECT ON THAT DAY:
RESURRECTION

When Jesus comes we expect to see him. In a flash he will finish the renewal of all things. The dead will be raised at his command. And his final judgment will be the climactic close of the world's history.

A True Picture?

It may be too simple to think that, by collecting the texts about the *parousia* from the pages of the New Testament, we can confidently conclude how Christ's coming will take place and what events will occur.

What if some people had studied the Old Testament Scriptures in order to say what would happen at the first coming of Christ—how accurate would their picture have been?

Certainly they would have expected the Redeemer of Israel, the Son of David, and they would have predicted his birth in Bethlehem. Yet the actual fulfillment in Jesus was an amazing surprise. Instead of a king, he turned out to be a carpenter. Instead of defeating his enemies, he died for them. Instead of liberating his people from the Romans, he saved them from sin.

We do have certain advantages over those who studied the Old Testament texts in expectation of his first coming. For one thing, we know for whom we are looking. "This same Jesus, who has been taken from you into heaven, will come back in the same way you have seen him go into heaven" (Acts 1:11). This *same* Jesus! Those who saw him will know him, but we will know him too. In fact, we have inside knowledge of Jesus Christ because we have his Spirit in our hearts and by that Spirit we pray for his coming (Rom. 8:9, 26). At the revelation of the Lord, our experience will undoubtedly surpass our expectations. What he will do and say will probably not follow the agenda we have composed in our books about his second coming. Yet Christ himself cannot be inconsistent with the Spirit he has given us, and his future actions will not contradict the Word he has left us.

The women who came to the grave to care for Jesus' corpse on that Sunday morning were told by the angel, "He is not here; he has risen, just as he said" (Matt. 28:6). There is a slight rebuke in that "just as he said." We may not forget or neglect what Christ told us, for he will certainly do what he said. His second coming will be different from our earthbound, time-conditioned imagination. No doubt. But when it happens it will be "just as he said."

We Will See His Glory

At last our faith will become sight and we will have the meeting about which the church of Christ has been singing and preaching for two thousand years or more. What will Christ look like? We find the last reliable report of someone who saw our Savior in Revelation 1:13-16. John saw, "someone 'like a son of man,' . . . his head and hair were white . . . his eyes were like blazing fire. His feet were like bronze glowing in a furnace, and his voice was like the sound of rushing waters. . . . out of his mouth came a sharp double-edged sword. His face was like the sun shining in all its brilliance."

This is the king of glory. Although he looks like a "son of man," a human being, his face is an explosion of light so that neither friend nor foe dares to set eyes on him (see Rev. 20:11). From his mouth comes the ultimate Word, a sword that cuts the world in two. And the feet of Jesus, the kneeling-bench of the nations, have the glow that one sees in the heart of a furnace. He is awesome.

This is a visionary and apocalyptic description, of course. And by reading this report we don't get much wiser as to the visual details of the glorified Jesus. But John's record warns us that the Christ whom we are going to meet comes to us from the other side, from God. The vision shows that our thoughts and our words are simply not adequate—not fit to frame the other reality. He will come to us in heavenly glory.

Recently someone said to me, "Maybe Jesus has come already; perhaps he lives among the poor in Africa or in Latin America." After all, this person said, the world's population was unaware of Christ's first coming. And who says that in his second coming he won't be equally incognito?

But the Bible makes the point, repeatedly and emphatically, that the second coming of Christ is a coming with glory! In that respect, the second coming forms a contrast with the first coming. The first is an appearance of grace that "brings salvation" (Titus 2:11). But the second is "the glorious appearing of our great God and Savior, Jesus Christ" (2:13). He descended in the form of a servant at his first coming, but when he returns, everyone will bow before him (Phil. 2:6-11). Throughout the New Testament, the humility and modesty of the first coming is contrasted with the exaltation and publicity of the second advent. When Jesus told his disciples that he had come to die on a cross, he contrasted this way of sorrows with another coming: "For the Son of Man is going to come in his Father's glory with his angels . . . " (Matt. 16:27). The first time he came to bear our sins, "and he will appear a second time, not to bear sin, but to bring salvation to those who are waiting for him" (Heb. 9:28).

In the Old Testament, "glory" is the radiance of God's holiness that people cannot bear and from which seraphs protect themselves with their wings

(Isa. 6). And the "Day of the Lord" is the final revelation of the power and holiness of God—a dreadful day for the wicked and glorious for his beloved. The New Testament states,

> [7]This will happen when the Lord Jesus is revealed from heaven in blazing fire with his powerful angels. [8]He will punish those who do not know God and do not obey the gospel of our Lord Jesus. [9]They will be punished with everlasting destruction and shut out from the presence of the Lord and from the majesty of his power [10]on the day he comes to be glorified in his holy people and to be marveled at among all those who have believed.
>
> —2 Thessalonians 1:7-10

Note that the glory of the Lord, which is a "blazing fire" for his enemies, is at the same time a radiance shared with his "holy people." At his coming we will see and share the glory of the Lord. And already in our present lives we have something of that glory of God.

We Will Be Like Jesus

We who have "received" Jesus (John 1:12) are now God's children. Our new life, the imperishable life, has started in us. That reality may be called the formation of a new person (John 3:3), the gift of the Holy Spirit himself (John 3:6; Rom. 5:5; 8:11, 16). It is the amazing gospel fact that we, here and now, may be called children of God. "And that is what we are!" exclaims the writer of 1 John 3:1—as if he himself can hardly believe it.

He continues, "Dear friends, now we are children of God, and what we will be has not yet been made known. But we know that when he appears, we shall be like him, for we shall see him as he is" (3:2).

"We shall be like him" does not imply equality with Jesus but likeness. We will share his immortality and his glorious life. With him we will live beyond the limitations of this present existence. Already we are God's children, but when we see him, we will (suddenly) reach completion, fullness.

Paul teaches the same thing: "For you died, and your life is now hidden with Christ in God. When Christ, who is your life, appears, then you also will appear with him in glory" (Col. 3:4). Our redeemed life does not exist apart from Christ. Christ is our life. In him we died to the old world; with him we arose to a new hope. But what we really are remains hidden as long as Christ is hidden. When he appears, the fullness of our new life will also appear.

When Jesus comes he will frighten whatever and whoever is opposed to God. But his coming will bring fruition and completion of everything and everybody born of his Spirit. Therefore "seeing him" in that day will be terror and sweetness.

He Will Come on the Clouds

Jesus will come as a human being with divine glory. That is also the meaning of the ancient expression, "one like a son of man, coming with the clouds of heaven" (Dan. 7:13). He is on our side because he is a child of our race. But he comes "with the clouds of heaven." And the clouds are really the chariot of God (Isa. 19:1; Ps. 104:3).

As I have said earlier, Jesus used to call himself "*the* Son of Man," not "*a* Son of Man." And in the hour when he was condemned to die, he prophesied, "In the future you will see the Son of Man sitting at the right hand of the Mighty One and coming on the clouds of heaven" (Matt. 26:64). Jesus confessed that he was the figure of Daniel 7:13.

At his second coming, he will be revealed on the clouds. That means he will be visible for all, and he will come with divine splendor. Even those who condemned him (Mark 14:64) and pierced him (Rev. 1:7) will see him and wail.

As long as he was with us, his glory was hidden behind weakness, sorrow, and his submission to death. He came as the sower to bring the kingdom (Matt. 13). He himself became the seed (John 12:23-26) that had to fall into the ground before the crop could be harvested. But when we see him again, he will come to harvest what he has sown: "before me was a white cloud, and seated on the cloud was one 'like a son of man' with a crown of gold on his head and a sharp sickle in his hand . . . " (Rev. 14:14).

And If We Die Before He Comes?

The earliest Christians pinned all their hope on meeting Jesus. And they expected Christ to wake up those who had already died, or "fallen asleep," as they said. One loud command of Christ would be enough.

But Jesus still has not come. And today's Christians talk much more about going to heaven and much less about waiting for resurrection day.

At death body and soul are wrenched apart. The soul departs and our body disintegrates—returns to dust, as the Bible says (Gen. 3:19). Almost all religions believe that people have these two parts: body and soul. Ancient religions had no problem believing that the soul could leave the body. What else happens in a dream? Isn't your spirit, or soul, wandering while your body remains in the room? Different religions place different values on the body and on the soul. All seem to agree that the soul (the spirit, or the inner life) is the more valuable part. But they regard the body as a temporary vehicle for the soul. A number of Asian religions teach that the soul must wander from one vehicle to another until it finds rest, like a river that empties into the ocean. The Greeks believed that the soul is immortal and that the body is its prison.

This belief is still popular. In California in March 1997, thirty-nine members of a cult called Heaven's Gate committed suicide by eating poisoned pudding and apple sauce. "By the time you read this, we will have exited our vehicles," said the suicide note. Their souls had "advanced to a higher level," they believed, and would be picked up by a spaceship.

In contrast to these beliefs, Christianity teaches that human beings form an entity, a body-soul unit. A body without the soul and a soul without a body are not really human beings. However, at death—at least, in the case of God's children—the soul, or spirit, goes to God or to Jesus. Our personal existence is continued between our death and the day of Jesus Christ, because God keeps us alive. In that sense the soul is immortal.

The Bible does not allow us to belittle the significance of the body:

- The body is part of God's good creation.

- The eternal Son of God assumed a human body and still has it.

- The value of the human body is especially underlined by the Bible's teaching of the resurrection of the body. This doctrine is uniquely and typically Christian. And the hope of the resurrection is at the heart of the Christian faith.

The Old Testament Expectation

In the Old Testament, life on earth is very important. Death is feared and hated because it cuts us off from life under the sun and puts us in the shade of Sheol—the place where dead people go. Long life is a blessing for those who fear God, but the wicked don't deserve it: "The fear of the LORD adds length to life, but the years of the wicked are cut short" (Prov. 10:27).

God gives us life to enjoy and to praise him. But "never again will [the dead] have part in anything that happens under the sun" (Eccles. 9:6). Besides, in Sheol, God is not praised. "No one remembers [God] when he is dead. Who praises you from the grave?" (Ps. 6:5).

Dying is the unavoidable end of all that lives on earth. And when the present life has been lived to the full, one ought to face facts with a certain resignation. "Now I am about to go the way of all the earth," said Joshua (Josh. 23:14). And David used the same words when his time had come (1 Kings 2:2).

Although the present life on earth seems to get all the emphasis in the Old Testament, it would be wrong to say that the Israelites had no hope for the afterlife.

In the first place, Israel knew that God is also Lord over death. In that sense death does not have the last word. Power to kill and to make alive belongs to

God (Deut. 32:39). And no one can escape the LORD, not even in the realm of the dead (Amos 9:1; Ps. 139:8).

In the second place, death may be a realm of darkness, a mist into which everyone disappears, but sometimes faith has moments of light:

- "My heart is glad and my tongue rejoices; my body also will rest secure, because you will not abandon me to the grave (Hebrew: *Sheol*), nor will you let your Holy One see decay" (Ps. 16:9-10).

- "God will redeem my life from the grave; he will surely take me to himself" (Ps. 49:15).

- "You guide me with your counsel, and afterward you will take me into glory" (Ps. 73:24).

In the third place, the Old Testament not only offers the personal hope of believers that their God has dominion over death, it also prophesies the destruction of death itself.

It is true that many "resurrection" prophecies refer to the restoration of Israel rather than to the final resurrection of the body: "But your dead will live; their bodies will rise" (Isa. 26:19); "O my people, I am going to open your graves and bring you up from them; I will bring you back to the land of Israel" (Ezek. 37:12).

And yet the vision that is at the heart of what we call "The Isaiah Apocalypse" (Isa. 24-27) is a prophecy quoted by Paul in 1 Corinthians 15. "On this mountain he will destroy the shroud that enfolds all peoples, the sheet that covers all nations; he will swallow up death forever. The Sovereign LORD will wipe away the tears from all faces" (Isa. 25:7-8). This is a prophecy of the universal shalom: the death of death and the future restoration of the goodness of God's creation.

Daniel 12:2 predicts that "multitudes (Hebrew: *many*) who sleep in the dust of the earth will awake; some to everlasting life, others to shame and everlasting contempt." This is a clear statement on the resurrection of the righteous and the wicked—the only clear one in the Old Testament. While it is not (yet) a teaching of a general resurrection, it does tell us that justice will be meted out to the dead, both to the righteous and to their oppressors.

The Teaching of the New Testament

The hope of Old Testament saints was focused on what God can do. The hope of New Testament believers is built on what God has already done in raising Jesus Christ from death. Resurrection is for us not merely a hope, it is a fact. Our gospel is good news precisely because we proclaim that Jesus is *alive*. He is victor, not victim, of death. He "has destroyed death and has brought life and immortality to light through the gospel" (2 Tim. 1:10), which the church proclaims.

For us resurrection is both a possession and a promise. In Christ we already have it. But personally we don't have it yet. The "firstfruits of those who have fallen asleep" (1 Cor. 15:20) has been raised already. On that peg we hang our hope: "God raised the Lord from the dead, and he will raise us also" (1 Cor. 6:14).

When Jesus reassured Martha, whose brother, Lazarus, had just died, "Your brother will rise again" (John 11:23), Martha responded, "I know he will rise again in the resurrection at the last day" (v. 24). That was her hope for the far-away future. But Jesus replied, "I am the resurrection and the life. He who believes in me will live, even though he dies; and whoever lives and believes in me will never die" (v. 25). What she expects in the future is here already.

The *already . . . but not yet* describes the tension in our faith and in our lives. The kingship of God is here already but we don't see it yet. We are holy already but we aren't quite sanctified yet. And we most strongly experience this *already . . . but not yet* when we face death. We have life and immortality, but we still carry our loved ones to the grave. We do not yet see the full victory of Jesus Christ. But the sting of death is gone already.

First Corinthians 15 is the great chapter about the resurrection that forms an integral part of the church's gospel. It begins in verses 1-11 with an impressive restatement of that gospel: "this is what we preach, and this is what you believed" (v. 11). In the rest of the chapter, Paul forcefully maintains *that* the dead are raised (v. 12) and then addresses the question of *how* they will be raised (v. 35).

Paul writes, "But someone may ask, 'How are the dead raised? With what kind of body will they come?' How foolish!" (Greek: *fool*). This sounds strange and discourteous to us, but in the Bible a fool is someone who does not know God. Paul is going to point out that our insight into this doctrine depends on our knowledge of God and the resources he has at his disposal:

> [36]What you sow does not come to life unless it dies. [37]When you sow, you do not plant the body that will be, but just a seed, perhaps of wheat or of something else. [38]But God gives it a body as he has deter-mined, and to each kind of seed he gives its own body. [39]All flesh is not the same: Men have one kind of flesh, animals have another, birds another and fish another. [40]There are also heavenly bodies and there are earthly bodies; but the splendor of the heavenly bodies is one kind, and the splendor of the earthly bodies is another. [41]The sun has one kind of splendor, the moon another and stars another; and star differs from star in splendor.

⁴²So will it be with the resurrection of the dead. The body that is sown is perishable, it is raised imperishable; ⁴³it is sown in dishonor, it is raised in glory; it is sown in weakness, it is raised in power; ⁴⁴it is sown a natural body, it is raised a spiritual body.

If there is a natural body, there is also a spiritual body. ⁴⁵So it is written: "The first man Adam became a living being"; the last Adam, a life-giving spirit. ⁴⁶The spiritual did not come first, but the natural, and after that the spiritual. ⁴⁷The first man was of the dust of the earth, the second man from heaven. ⁴⁸As was the earthly man, so are those who are of the earth; and as is the man from heaven, so also are those who are of heaven. ⁴⁹And just as we have borne the likeness of the earthly man, so shall we bear the likeness of the man from heaven.

—1 Corinthians 15:36-49

If you have trouble believing in the resurrection of the human body—and who doesn't?—go with the apostle Paul and see how seed must go into the ground and "die" before God gives it another body. Learn two things from Paul: the seed must be "buried" or "sown" before the other body can come forth. And the body that comes out of the ground is quite different from the one that goes into it.

Many argue that Paul also means to teach a continuity between the seed that is sown and the body that is reaped, because he states that "to each kind of seed he gives its own body" (v. 38). But I don't believe that's a point he is making here.

Paul wants us to see the enormous variety of "bodies" that God creates in this world. A kernel goes into the earth and a six-foot high cornstalk comes out. Look at the variety of plants and trees! In his sovereign freedom, God gives to each seed that goes into the ground its own body. Also people, animals, fish, and fowl have different "flesh." Each has its own manner of existence in this present world. That's how incredibly rich and inexhaustible God's resources are.

This great variety and power is not limited to what we see on earth. There are also heavenly bodies that have a splendor that differs from the splendor of the earthly bodies. And the heavenly bodies don't all have the same radiance. The glory of the sun differs from the glory of the moon, and the splendor of stars differs from each other (vv. 37-41).

The apostle points to all these bodies that the sovereign God has sown and created. Paul makes us almost dizzy as we try to follow his outstretched hand, pointing at bodies on earth and in the sky—all different, a vast exhibition of God's freedom, power, and creativity. And then Paul adds: "So will it be with the resurrection of the dead" (v. 42). He has been lecturing us about the possibility and procedure of the resurrection of the body. That's why he made us look at seeds that fell into the ground and the totally different bodies that resulted from this process. That's why he showed us bodies on earth and bodies in heaven. And that's why he has already dropped the word *glory* or *splendor*.

Now he makes the transition from the comparison of the seed to the contrast between the heavenly and the earthly man. He makes this move through a fourfold comparison of great literary power (vv. 42-44):

SOWN	RAISED
perishable	imperishable
dishonor	glory
weakness	power
a natural body	a spiritual body

With this last contrast, the whole comparison is hooked up to Adam and Christ. Adam gave us the natural (Greek: *psychic*) body and from Christ we shall receive a spiritual (Greek: *pneumatic*) body. For, according to Genesis 2:7, Adam became a living being (*psyche*), but after his resurrection, Christ became a life-giving Spirit (*pneuma*) (see 2 Cor. 3:17-18).

First comes the natural, then comes the spiritual (1 Cor. 15:44), meaning that the last Adam who gives the Spirit comes after the first Adam. And we too, after having lived in Adam-like fashion, will be reshaped in the image of the last Adam, Christ, the Spiritual One. With Adam, Eve, and all their children, we turn to dust. With Christ and all who belong to him, we receive the Spirit and a resurrection body.

The Spiritual Body

A spiritual body is still a *body*. We are not going to be disembodied ghosts. *Spiritual* is not the opposite of *material*. When we have a spiritual body we are no longer weak, sinful, mortal. The resurrection body is called *spiritual* because its existence is completely qualified by the Holy Spirit. To a certain extent, we are already spiritual. But our existence is not yet fully controlled by the Spirit of God. However, "if the Spirit of him who raised Jesus from the dead is living in you, he who raised Christ from the dead will also give life to your mortal bodies through his Spirit, who lives in you" (Rom. 8:11). Then we will be completely fit to live with the Lord.

It is necessary for everybody to be changed before we can enter the kingdom—the realm that is totally dominated by the presence of God. The change begins with conversion. It begins with a new heart, a new desire, and a new hope. But it won't be complete until we have new bodies and live on a new earth. The final change takes place either by death and resurrection or "in a flash, in the twinkling of an eye, at the last trumpet" (1 Cor. 15:52). But change we must! We must not only have a clean heart but also an imperishable body. That is the purpose of the redemption for which Christ is now working.

We will have a body like the one Jesus has had since his resurrection. You will still be you and I will still be me. There will be continuity and change. We won't find that continuity in some seed or DNA that remains of our present bodies but in the power of God to raise us from death. The change will be in the newness: we will be delivered from sin and from its consequences. The blind will see, the lame will leap, the tone-deaf will sing.

People always ask if we will recognize each other. And nobody knows. Recognition is dependent on memory. And I think that God will graciously erase our memory banks. Yet we will know the Lord and each other better than ever.

The "Thinkability" of the Resurrection

The most unique biblical teaching is the resurrection of the body and it is the hardest doctrine to believe. Before the coming of Christ, the Sadducees denied it and the Pharisees taught it. Jesus said the Pharisees were right (Matt. 22:23f.). Paul cleverly used the disagreement between Pharisees and Sadducees when he stood before the Sanhedrin (Acts 23:6-10). When he was on trial before Felix, Paul again attempted to shift attention to the dispute about the resurrection (Acts 24:21).

Paul brought the gospel to Athens. The Greeks seemed to listen to him with interest but "when they heard about the resurrection of the dead, some of them sneered . . . " (Acts 17:32). Even within the church of Corinth some people apparently denied the resurrection of believers, even though they seemed to accept the fact that Jesus arose (1 Cor. 15:12). Perhaps these Corinthian Christians held the same teaching which Hymenaeus and Philetus were spreading in Ephesus: "They say that the resurrection has already taken place, and they destroy the faith of some" (2 Tim. 2:18). Hymenaeus and Philetus must have taught a spiritual resurrection, not a literal resurrection of the body.

Paul yields no ground. In 1 Corinthians 15 he argues that it is the resurrection or nothing.

In the contemporary Christian church, the resurrection of the body is not denied but is certainly neglected. For most people the issue is "whether you'll go to heaven when you die." The assumption is that the body is for the worms but the soul goes to heaven or hell.

The Bible doesn't say it's *not* so, but it certainly does not formulate this big issue in that manner.

For Paul the issue is "to know Christ and the power of his resurrection and the fellowship of sharing in his sufferings, becoming like him in his death, and so, somehow, to attain to the resurrection from the dead" (Phil. 3:10-11). Our goal for every day is more of Christ and less of self. And our ultimate goal is the resurrection of the body.

Paul never excludes the body when he thinks of the future. So we may not deprecate the body in our present form of existence. "The body is not meant for sexual immorality, but for the Lord, and the Lord for the body" (1 Cor. 6:13). The body is intended for the Lord's service, just as the Lord gave himself in service for our bodies. He identified himself bodily with our weaknesses; he died our physical death. "By his power God raised the Lord from the dead, and he will raise us also. Do you not know that your bodies are members of Christ himself? Shall I then take the members of Christ and unite them with a prostitute? Never!" (1 Cor. 6:14-15).

The moral issue, sexual sin, is cast in the framework of Christ's redemption of our bodies by his first and second coming. He came and made us his own. Therefore we cannot give our bodies to anyone else. "You are not your own; you were bought at a price. Therefore honor God with your body" (vv. 19-20). And just as Christ identified with us in our weak body, so we shall be raised and be with him and like him. Our bodies are for the Lord!

The resurrection may help us make the future more "thinkable." We will be in the body. For, as we have seen, a spiritual body is not the opposite of a material body. A spiritual body is the opposite of what is perishable, dishonorable, weak, natural. The transformation of the body begins here and now when I offer my body as a living sacrifice to God (Rom. 12:1). It happens when I don't allow my present way of living in the body to be conformed to this world. If and when this bodily life of ours is being transformed by the newness that we have from God's Holy Spirit, it becomes a prelude of the bodily life we will enjoy in the future (see Rom. 12:1-2).

The Heart of Our Hope

The denial or neglect of the resurrection of the body destroys practical piety and results in a hazy kind of holiness.

Our ignoring of the resurrection may be related to our inability to imagine this biblical teaching. Let's face it: our ancestors "fell asleep" awaiting the resurrection, the "great gettin'-up morning." They believed that the angel with his trumpet would act as God's alarm clock and that God himself had set the timer. But there is nothing left of our ancestors. Nothing. And times are rolling on. Therefore, the idea that the soul goes to heaven when the body goes to "nothing" is a more "thinkable" doctrine. And there is some biblical support for it.

However, the heart of the Christian gospel beats in the teaching concerning the resurrection of the body. Why? Because this gospel is the announcement that the old age has died and the new age has begun in the death and resurrection of Jesus Christ. We are already living with one leg out of the grave. Death is a monster but its claws are cut, its sting removed. Just a little while and everything will be fresh and strong. The firstfruits have been harvested.

Christians are people who meet on Sunday because that's their birthdate. On the first day of the week, we were born again to a living hope (1 Pet. 1:3). And this is the kind of indestructible life that we want to see perfected. That's why we must have the resurrection of the dead. The body-for-the-worms-and-the-soul-to-Christ is no solution. It stalls the process of our full salvation,

---

The "intermediate state," that is, our condition during the time between our physical death and the resurrection of the body, receives only indirect attention in the Scriptures. Whenever one of our loved ones dies, we ask numerous questions about where he or she is, if she is conscious, if he can see us, and so forth. In funeral homes we tend to comfort each other with fantasies about heaven, saying what we would like to believe rather than what we actually know. We ought to admit that we cannot answer most questions about the state of the departed, simply because God has not told us.

The texts about the intermediate state are few in number:

- "I tell you the truth, today you will be with me in paradise" (Luke 23:43). This is one of Jesus' well-known sayings from the cross. Christ promised an early meeting—*today*—with the thief who hung next to him. The meeting would occur in a place of bliss called paradise.

- When our life is Christ, our dying will be gain. At times we can understand Paul's "desire to depart and be with Christ, which is better by far" (Phil. 1:23). When he says "depart and be with Christ," Paul refers to a move from the present address to the other one.

- Paul also speaks of this in 2 Corinthians 5:8, "[We] would prefer to be away from the body and at home with the Lord." From such expressions we learn that Paul did not believe in a prolonged state of unconsciousness between death and resurrection, as some people teach.

- The parable about the rich man and Lazarus should not be used, I believe, to draw any sort of map of the scenery after death. By it the Lord does tell us that death, and the great divide after death, is coming, and that we are well-advised to keep it in mind while we live our present lives.

- Although there is much uncertainty concerning the kind of life (or death) we will experience when we disappear behind the curtain, there

although the Bible assures us that this intermediate state won't put us in a void and won't let us fall out of God's hand.

For our limited intellect, this resurrection is impossible to imagine. Therefore we must keep following Paul's advice and walk in creation and scan the heavens. Creation is a book full of pictures about God. God's power and creativity are overwhelming. And yet we receive the *real* foretaste of the future by knowing Christ. What God is doing right now through the last Adam, pushing for a renewed creation, is so great that we need all the sciences and all the saints if we want to begin to measure it.

is one overpowering, crucial consideration that makes us sure of our continued personal existence with the Lord. It is the consideration of the faithfulness of God himself. When Jesus argued with the Sadducees, who did not appear to believe in any sort of afterlife, he told them that they did not know the Scriptures nor the power of God. Then he taught them about our continued life after death with a text you or I would never have used. Had they not read that God said to Moses, "I am the God of Abraham, the God of Isaac, and the God of Jacob? He is not the God of the dead, but of the living" (Mark 12:26-27). In Luke 20:38 Jesus adds, "for to him all are alive."

Once God has established a covenantal bond with Abraham—or with you or me—it is necessarily an eternal communion. We covenant with each other as marriage partners and our vows are binding until death parts us. But death never parts us from the living God. Neither death nor any other calamity "will be able to separate us from the love of God that is in Christ Jesus our Lord" (Rom. 8:39). If we know the Scriptures and the power of God, we realize that all who die in Christ are alive to him.

This teaching of a conscious life with God after death and before the resurrection of the body has formed part of the confessions of the Christian church since the beginning. (See, for instance, Lord's Day 22 of the Heidelberg Catechism as discussed in my commentary *Comfort & Joy: A Study of the Heidelberg Catechism*, pp. 146-151.)

There are numerous theological and philosophical questions and debates concerning the body, the soul, and the relationship between the two—what constitutes a person and how she or he can continue to exist after death. For an up-to-date discussion see John W. Cooper, *Body, Soul, and Life Everlasting: Biblical Anthropology and the Monism-Dualism Debate.*

The Last Judgment

—Peter Paul Reubens, 1577-1640

CHAPTER 13

WHAT WE EXPECT ON THAT DAY:
THE NEW EARTH AND FINAL JUDGMENT

The Liberation of Creation

In the last chapter, we looked at the unique Christian teaching of the resurrection of our bodies that will occur when Christ returns. But that's not all that we expect to happen on that day. The Bible says that not only our bodies but the whole earth is in God's redemptive program, although we are not given a systematic presentation of this program.

We find the first reference to the promise of the new earth in Isaiah 65:17 and 66:22. That expectation endures in the New Testament (2 Pet. 3:13) and the Bible closes with that vision in Revelation 21. Actually it speaks there not only of a new earth, but of a "new heaven and a new earth" (v. 1). By *heaven* we should think of what we call the atmospheric heavens—what we see when we look up. Heaven as "the abode of the glorified saints" is different. That heaven "needs no renewal because it is unaffected by sin" (Simon J. Kistemaker, *New Testament Commentary: Peter and Jude,* p. 340).

This raises the question of what will happen to the old earth. Will it be annihilated and will God then create a new heaven and earth out of nothing? The Bible speaks of terrible things that must happen to the old heaven and earth. On the day of the Lord, when God will deal with his enemies, his terrible wrath will be poured out. The world as we know it collapses: "The LORD is angry with all the nations. . . . He will totally destroy them . . . the mountains will be soaked with their blood. All the stars of the heavens will be dissolved and the sky rolled up like a scroll; all the starry host will fall like withered leaves from the vine" (Isa. 34:2-4).

The extinction of the heavenly lights and the writhing of a dark and bloody earth are stock features of the apocalyptic pictures of the end (see Ezek. 32; Joel 2-3). These visions recur in the New Testament, first in the speech of Jesus about the destruction of Jerusalem and the return of the Son of Man (Mark 13:24f.) and also in the book of Revelation.

Second Peter 3 tells us that, just as the earth God first created was destroyed by water, so "the present heavens and earth are reserved for fire" (2 Pet. 3:7). When the day of the Lord comes, "the heavens will disappear with a roar; the elements will be destroyed by fire, and the earth and everything in it will be laid bare" (v. 10).

The text of 2 Peter 3:10 is a difficult one. It speaks of the destruction of the heavens, which will "pass away with a rushing sound" or "disappear with a roar." The

Beginning in 1945, the King James Version of 2 Peter 3:10 became the springboard for nuclear war predictions in the dispensational premil camps. It reads, "But the day of the Lord will come as a thief in the night; in which the heavens shall pass away with a great noise, and the elements shall melt with fervent heat, the earth also and the works that are therein shall be burned up."

In August 1945, President Harry Truman announced the destruction of Hiroshima and Nagasaki by atomic bombs. In November 1945 *Moody Monthly* announced, with obvious satisfaction, "The Bible is ahead of science again." An atomic blast shows an "exact picture" of what 2 Peter 3:10 described many centuries ago. Soon the prophecy pundits found nuclear weapons and thermonuclear blasts throughout the Bible. The bombs, the missiles, and the destruction of millions were all described by Ezekiel, Joel, Zephaniah, and in the Apocalypse of John. (This development is thoroughly researched and entertainingly told by Paul Boyer, *When Time Shall Be No More,* pp. 115-151.)

The dangerous and, yes, sinful trend in this sensational writing and preaching was that Christians sanctioned the arms race during the cold war. They claimed that God *intended* the world to suffer a nuclear holocaust. They predicted failure for peace talks and arms control. At one time it seemed that president Ronald Reagan believed that "Armageddon" would be the God-intended end of the cold war. Some of his advisers preached that there was a link between "our" weapons and God's plan (Boyer, p. 140f.).

"elements" that will be destroyed through fire or heat have nothing to do with physical or chemical elements; they are the celestial bodies: sun, moon, and stars. This text echoes what other apocalyptic sayings about the end have stated: that the atmospheric heaven will disappear and the heavenly lights will go out.

The last clause of verse 10 is unclear. The earth and the works it contains "will be burned up" (KJV), or "will be laid bare" (NIV, NEB), or "will be disclosed" (NRSV).

The first heaven and the first earth will pass away. Then we expect the new heaven and the new earth on which righteousness dwells. In Revelation 21 John says that he saw the new heaven and earth after the first had passed away. We may not underestimate the righteous judgments of God that have come and that will come over this rebellious cosmos. But God will not annihilate the works of his own hands. A new creation *ex nihilo,* "out of nothing"—a totally new beginning—would not only be inconsistent with several Bible texts, but also with the faithfulness of God as we know God.

A completely new earth unrelated to the present one would also be inconsistent with the Bible's teaching on the resurrection of the body. If our *bodies* have a future, the *earth* has a future. Just as our present bodies function only on this earth, which God created and sustains, so our new bodies will function in the renewed environment of the recreated earth. When God makes something new, the old is not discarded but perfected. That holds true for the new (Greek: *kainos*) covenant (Luke 22:20), the new (*kainos*) commandment (John 13:34), and for the new (*kainos*) heaven and the new earth (Rev. 21:1). The new is what the old was intended to become.

That's why Paul calls the new earth the liberated cosmos. In Romans 8:19 he does not picture the present creation as fleeing from the wrath of God as John does in Revelation 16 when the seventh angel pours out the bowl of wrath. He pictures it as a deer that pricks up its ears or as a dog that hears its master coming. And what is creation so eagerly awaiting? The revelation of the sons of God! Creation wants to see the new humanity, our resurrected bodies. When we fell from our high calling as God's appointed stewards of creation (Gen. 3), the whole creation was incarcerated in a prison of corruption. And the liberation of creation will be no sooner and no later than the day when we human beings are totally free and altogether redeemed (Rom. 8:19-21).

Our outlook and our work should be determined by the perspective of Romans 8. The salvation, not the destruction, of creation is the goal of our work. The hope of the resurrection of the body is wedded to the restoration of creation. That hope pervades the world and beats in our hearts by the Holy Spirit (v. 23). Creation pricks up its ears and we lift up our hearts to the One who is coming.

The Final Judgment

Judgment follows the resurrection. In some sense it also precedes the resurrection. John 3:18 tells us that the Son of God's love has come into the world and that "whoever believes in him is not condemned, but whoever does not believe stands condemned already because he has not believed in the name of God's one and only Son." But someday that judgment must become public (John 5:29).

People often ask why there has to be a final judgment if our eternal destiny is already decided when we die. We believe that all who die in the Lord will be with the Lord until he brings them with him in the day of his appearing. Why then a day of judgment? Because that's the way it's pictured in the Bible. And, as we saw, we know very little about the intermediate state. The Bible focuses our attention on that day when we are raised from the dead and physically able to stand before the judgment seat, together with those who are still alive when the Lord returns, who will be changed in the twinkling of an eye.

The Purpose of the Final Judgment

The main purpose for Judgment Day is the glory of God and of his Son. We are inclined to think that the Last Judgment will finally reveal our eternal destiny. But that's not its purpose. Our final destiny is the end of the road on which we are traveling *today*.

When Christ is revealed as the Judge of the living and the dead, he will receive cosmic recognition and universal acclaim. That's the main idea. Everyone who ever lived in God's world will finally admit that God is our Creator and Judge and that we are, in the most literal sense of the word, at his mercy.

The last judgment is the day on which justice will be finally and fully done. Without that final judgment, history would have no meaning. In the present dispensation, weeds and wheat grow together in God's field and it is not our task to separate them from each other. But in the end, that separation will be done by the Son of Man and his angels (Matt. 13:24-30, 36-43). It is not right that in the present life the meek are shoved aside by the arrogant and the poor are oppressed by the rich. Christians know that oppressors are fattening themselves for the day of slaughter (James 5:1-6). We do not seek revenge. That belongs to the Lord (Rom. 12:19), and sometimes to the courts (Rom. 13:4). In spite of the police, the courts, and the armies, villains still seem to get away with murder, especially the ones who are well-connected. But no one will get away with it forever. Everyone has to appear before God. Otherwise history is meaningless. That's why the psalmist delights in the expectation of that day:

Then all the trees of the forest will sing for joy;
they will sing before the LORD, for he comes,
he comes to judge the earth.
He will judge the world in righteousness
and the peoples in his truth.
—Psalm 96:12-13

The Date Is Set, the Judge Appointed

From the time of the calling of Abraham (Gen. 12) until the day of Pentecost (Acts 2), most nations lived in ignorance and sin. But God "overlooked it." In other words, he did not punish them as they deserved: "In the past God overlooked such ignorance, but now he commands all people everywhere to repent. For he has set a day when he will judge the world with justice by the man he has appointed. He has given proof of this to all men by raising him from the dead" (Acts 17:30-31).

The worldwide mission program has been launched and all nations must now repent. The date for judgment has been set. God alone knows that date, and he will keep the appointment. Jesus of Nazareth is the agent through whom he will judge. God first vindicated Jesus in the resurrection. The One who was rejected by his own and crucified by the Romans was raised by God on the third day. God has declared, "You are my Son; today I have become your Father. Ask of me, and I will make the nations your inheritance, the ends of the earth your possession" (Ps. 2:7-8). The Father will publicly and cosmically vindicate his Son on Judgment Day.

So Jesus is the Judge. "We must all appear before the judgment seat of Christ . . . " (2 Cor. 5:10).

It's no contradiction, of course, that the New Testament also teaches that God is the Judge, for there is no contradiction between the Father and the Son. We have no idea how the work of judgment will be carried out. And we should not use a mental image of some famous trial as an example, either consciously or subconsciously. Our judicial trials deal mainly with investigation. But the last judgment will involve mainly publication and execution (A. A. Hoekema, *The Bible and the Future*, p. 254).

Church members will have a role in the final judgment. According to 1 Corinthians 6:3, "we will judge angels." Those must be fallen angels (Jude 6). We receive no further information, only the admonition that if God has such a job in mind for us, we'd better show ourselves to be competent in adjudicating the trivial cases that arise among us (1 Cor. 6:2).

The twelve apostles will receive a special assignment: "I tell you the truth, at the renewal of all things, when the Son of Man sits on his glorious throne, you who have followed me will also sit on twelve thrones, judging the twelve tribes of Israel" (Matt. 19:28). But "judging" here may also mean "governing."

The "Thinkability" of the Last Judgment

We must not be afraid to admit that we have no idea how God will take care of the logistics of the final judgment. Leave it to God! We should certainly not fall into the error of the premil dispensationalists, who schedule at least two judgments, usually four, and sometimes even more than that.

The last judgment is out of our time zones. Everything that happens at the *parousia* and after it, will be . . . well . . . different. When Christ comes, we will pass the border between our time and our earthbound existence into . . . *what?* It will be a new form of existence and a different manner of living. We have no words and images for it, because all our words and images make sense only among flesh-and-blood earthlings. The Bible is written in words and symbols that make sense to this-worldly people. The words and symbols that are on the edge of our understanding, that are supposed to say something about the great future, we call *eschatological* and *apocalyptic*. They are more indications than descriptions. They are more signs than the things signified.

Should We Fear It?

There are some scary things about the last judgment. All the covers will be removed. There's "nothing concealed that will not be known or brought out into the open" (Luke 8:17). We "will have to give account on the day of judgment for every careless word [we] have spoken" (Matt. 12:36). And it will not be according to our opinions but by our deeds that we will be judged. Each of us will receive what is our due "for the things done while in the body, whether good or bad" (2 Cor. 5:10).

The removal of the covers also involves prayers offered in the inner room, for "your Father, who sees what is done in secret, will reward you" (Matt. 6:6). And the "cup of cold water" we give to Jesus' little ones will not be forgotten (Matt. 10:42).

The day is the occasion for handing out rewards. Some of us will receive nothing. Our works of faith were wrongly directed, ill conceived, badly executed. "It is burned up, he will suffer loss; he himself will be saved, but only as one escaping through the flames" (1 Cor. 3:15). And another one will hear, "You have been faithful with a few things; I will put you in charge of many things" (Matt. 25:21, 23).

The Lord intends thoughts of the last day to have a restraining influence on us. In the Bible God stoops to scare us with the last judgment and also encourages us with the prospect of gaining rewards in the hereafter. These are the eternally Wise One's methods to bring us to himself. We must not try to be too sophisticated for such threats and promises.

But the main thing we need to remember is that Jesus is the Judge. He is the same Jesus who died for us. So we may live with assurance of salvation, knowing that nothing can "separate us from the love of God that is in Christ Jesus our Lord" (Rom. 8:39). Yet the man who first wrote these words worked at self-discipline as if he had to earn his salvation: "I do not run like a man running aimlessly; I do not fight like a man beating the air. No, I beat my body and make it my slave so that after I have preached to others, I myself will not be disqualified for the prize" (1 Cor. 9:26-27).

Trusting Jesus and his accomplished work, we are sure we will be saved. But in the parable of the sheep and the goats (Matt. 25:31-46), in which the saved enter eternal life and the condemned eternal punishment, both groups receive their verdict with amazement. The certainty of salvation is always accompanied by amazement. For we are saved by grace.

Unbelievers and God's Enemies

The Bible says practically nothing about the resurrection of unbelievers. The passages in the letters of Paul that deal most directly with the resurrection of the body (1 Cor. 15; 1 Thess. 4) speak exclusively about the resurrection of Christians. As we have seen, Daniel 12:2 speaks of a resurrection of "multitudes" who sleep in the dust of the earth. Some will awake "to everlasting life, others to shame and everlasting contempt." In John 5:28-29 Jesus speaks of a general resurrection: "A time is coming when all who are in their graves will hear [the Son of Man's] voice and come out—those who have done good will rise to live, and those who have done evil will rise to be condemned." And in Acts 24:15 we read, "I have the same hope in God as these men, that there will be a resurrection of both the righteous and the wicked." These are the only texts that clearly state that the wicked will be raised from the dead. But they're enough.

People will be judged according to the light they received in this life. Those who were close to the mighty works of God in Christ—the people of Korazin, Bethsaida, Capernaum, and the city where I live—will be judged more severely for their unbelief than those who did not see and hear what we have seen and heard: Tyre, Sidon, and Sodom (Matt. 11:20-24).

Those who don't have God's inscripturated revelation will be judged by what they have done with the revelation of God in creation and in every human heart (Rom. 1:18-23; 2:12-16; Acts 14:17; 17:27).

The wicked will be raised from death and will be judged by God. His is the judgment, not ours. And as Abraham said, "Will not the Judge of all the earth do right?" (Gen. 18:25). But Abraham said it while he was pleading for Sodom and Gomorrah.

Hell and Eternal Punishment

There have been times when preachers and painters wallowed in sermons and pictures of unquenchable hell-fire, worms that did not die, and people in justly deserved, never-ending torment. But in our times the topic is almost taboo.

Many Christians believe in an ultimate, universal salvation, for God is love and he must be victorious. Even more Christians now believe what some sects have always taught: that God will annihilate the wicked. This view, in the form of *conditional immortality,* is becoming a popular teaching to which even some evangelical teachers subscribe. Their reasoning goes like this: We do not have immortality in ourselves. Immortality is a gift that God grants after death. God withholds this gift from the wicked, either at the time of their death or at the last judgment. If and when God so chooses, people simply cease to exist. These teachers harmonize annihilation with Scripture by saying that "eternal punishment" does not mean an act of punishment that goes on forever and anew, but it means an act of punishment that has irreversible results.

We would be bad human beings and worse Christians if we did not feel the desire for all people to be saved (universalism). God himself has that desire. Yet I cannot draw that conclusion from the texts cited by the universalists (Rom. 11:32, 36; 1 Cor. 15:24-28; Eph. 1:10; Col. 1:20) because they quote Paul out of context, ignoring the rest of what Paul wrote and did.

As for conditional immortality, it is easy to understand why people today are so attracted to this theory that we used to condemn. We are now much closer to adherents of other religions. We rub shoulders with those who refuse to accept Jesus Christ. They now live among us and we among them. We all live in a global village. Our thinking about the eternal lot of the "wicked" is no longer impersonal. Besides, what purpose could be served by an everlasting punishment in a torture chamber, when the new world has come in which God is all in all?

Of course these are emotional or philosophical considerations, and we must frame our faith by what the Bible actually teaches. Jesus speaks of a "hell of fire" and a road that "leads to destruction" right in his Sermon on the Mount (Matt. 5:22, 29, 30; 7:13). Christ warns that we must not fear those who can destroy the body. We must fear God, "who can destroy both body and soul in hell" (Matt. 10:28). *Hell* is the place "where 'their worm does not die, and the fire is not quenched'" (Mark 9:48, quoting from Isaiah 66:24). The servant who refused to use his talent in the service of his master was thrown into "the darkness, where there will be weeping and gnashing of teeth" (Matt. 25:30). And there is much more about hell and eternal punishment in the New Testament.

When the New Testament speaks about unbelievers who *perish* and about a road or a way of life that leads to *destruction,* responsible exegesis has always maintained that these words do not mean annihilation, but everlasting misery. These terms are used in opposition to everlasting life and joy. (See A. A. Hoekema, *The Bible and the Future,* ch. 19.)

The Bible does not describe a literal hell, of course. The worm and the fire are figures of speech for inner and outer anguish. Outer darkness symbolizes utter loneliness, being far from God. Weeping and gnashing of teeth stand for remorse and anger. The place is called *Gehenna,* which was the garbage dump near Jerusalem on desecrated ground where once children were sacrificed to Molech. Here the fire never stopped burning.

By means of the pictures of torment God makes us understand something of the ultimate seriousness of our being for him or against him. God warns us about an ultimate danger, and at the same time God extends to us an invitation to infinite blessing. In the words of Hebrews 10:28-31, "Anyone who rejected the law of Moses died without mercy on the testimony of two or three witnesses. How much more severely do you think a man deserves to be punished who has trampled the Son of God under foot, who has treated as an unholy thing the blood of the covenant that sanctified him, and who has insulted the Spirit of grace? . . . It is a dreadful thing to fall into the hands of the living God" (Heb. 10:28-31).

We are left with many questions. We ought to distrust those who claim they have all the answers. We must trust God because God is much wiser, more merciful and loving than any one of us. And it pleases God not to answer certain questions.

When someone asked Jesus, "Lord, are only a few people going to be saved?" Christ said in effect, That's none of your business; but you should "strive to enter through the narrow door" (Luke 13:24, NRSV).

A Feast

To live with God and all God's children on the new earth will be supreme happiness. It is difficult to imagine such a life. I tend to think of the happiest experiences in the present and then fancy them to last forever. The Bible instructs us to think in that manner, I think. Many biblical invitations to God's salvation urge us to attend a banquet or a wedding feast, the happiest moments in the lives of the people who lived in the villages of Palestine:

- God prepares "a feast of rich food for all peoples, a banquet of aged wine— the best of meats and the finest of wines" (Isa. 25:6).

- God beckons: "Come all you who are thirsty, come to the waters; and you who have no money, come, buy and eat! Come, buy wine and milk without money and without cost" (Isa. 55:1).

- "He has taken me to the banquet hall, and his banner over me is love" (Song of Songs 2:4).

- The great invitation to the kingdom in Jesus's parables is an invitation to a banquet (Luke 14:16) or a wedding feast (Matt. 22:2).

- When the lost sheep, the lost coin, and the lost son have been found, the celebrations begin (Luke 15).

- The ten virgins were waiting to attend the wedding celebration (Matt. 25:1-13).

- The servants who were faithful in their stewardship of their master's money are told to enter into "the joy of your master" (Matt. 25:21, 23, NRSV).

- When the end has come, a great multitude sings a hallelujah chorus: "For the wedding of the Lamb has come, and his bride has made herself ready" (Rev. 19:7).

To be with the Lord is a feast! We will be intensely happy. Everything that now curbs our joy will be removed. Whatever limits our happiness will be eradicated. "You will fill me with joy in your presence, with eternal pleasures at your right hand" (Ps. 16:11).

Scripture speaks of our happiness in physical and spiritual terms. We will be joyful because the pain, poverty, hunger, thirst, and cold of this life will be over. All the weakness, dishonor, error, sin and its consequences will be past. "And God will wipe every tear from their eyes" (Rev. 7:17; see also 21:4). We will be holy as God is holy. We will be glorious as Jesus is glorious. And our fellowship with him will be consummated.

That's another point made by the image of the wedding of the church and the Lamb. Our fellowship with him will be richer and deeper than it could ever be on the present earth. There will be no distance between us and no disturbance of that fellowship. Our unity with Christ and with God will no longer be mediated by the Bible or by the book of creation. It will be forever *im*mediate.

Restored to God

On that day Christ will have conquered all his enemies and ours. As we saw earlier, Christ has already won the battle, but the war is not yet over. Christ already has all authority (Matt. 28:18). God has already invited the Messiah to "sit at my right hand until I make your enemies a footstool for your feet" (Ps. 110:1; Acts 2:34). Jesus "sits on a royal throne." That means that he reigns until the last enemy bows and falls. The last enemy of his—and ours—that will be destroyed is death (1 Cor. 15:26). Then there will be peace. Christ will say to his Father: the harmony is restored, all things and all people bow before you. That will complete Christ's mediatorial work. "Then the Son himself will be made subject to him who put everything under him, so that God may be all in all" (1 Cor. 15:28).

Christ will not cease to be what he is, but he will stop doing what he did. No longer will he need to equip and lead his church to fight God's enemies. God will have no enemies anymore, and we will be home with our Father God. God will be "all in all"—totally supreme for everyone and everything. From God we come, by God we live, to God we are going. The real life is the God-centered life. God is our root and God is our sunlight. God will be the environment in which we will bloom forever.

Revelation 21 and 22

The last two chapters of Revelation give no literal description of our future home. Yet these visions of John have the power to make us homesick for Jerusalem.

In his vision John beholds the new heaven and the new earth. Gone is the first earth and gone is the sea. Ever since the flood the sea has posed the threat to the dry land. It stands for the forces of chaos, which would destroy the cosmos if God did not hold them back (see, for example, Ps. 93:3; 104:6-9). In the book of Revelation the sea also represents the political turmoil of the nations out of which the beast arises (Rev. 13). But now the sea is no more. That means that the last threat to our existence on this green earth under the friendly, starry heavens has been removed. Peace at last! All catastrophes, tornadoes, earthquakes, and crop failures are of the past. "God will again see what He has made, and He will declare that it is good with a goodness that cannot be destroyed" (Harry R. Boer, *The Book of Revelation*, p. 145).

The remainder of the vision does not concentrate on the renewed universe but on the new city, Jerusalem. God is not only the architect and builder of this city (Heb. 11:10, 16; 12:22), but God also dwells in it together with his own people. God and his people inhabit the new world; the borders between heaven and earth no longer exist (Rev. 21:3). This is the climax of the ever-closer communion between God and his people. In the Old Covenant, God lived with them in tabernacle and temple. But the Holy of Holies could be approached only by the high priest once a year. In the new dispensation, God's congregation itself became the temple, because the Holy Spirit dwelled in all who were purchased by the blood of Christ. In the new city God and his people live together. Heaven and earth meet in Jerusalem. The city and the temple are one and the same. There is no longer a difference between the cultus and culture, between worship and work, Sunday and Monday. Jerusalem is beautiful. Built in the form of a cube about 1,500 miles on each side (v. 16), it's modeled after the Most Holy Place of the tabernacle. The gates have the names of the twelve tribes, the foundations have the names of the twelve apostles. "The wall was jasper, the color of Glory, and the city was pure gold, translucent as glass" (Eugene H. Peterson, *The Message*). The foundations are garnished with gems, and every one of the twelve gates consists of a single pearl.

The greatest treasures of the realm of nature are used as images of the glory of Jerusalem. Other images are derived from paradise, with its tree of life (Rev. 21:6; 22:1-2) or from Ezekiel's river of life and temple vision. But the glory of the new will outshine all the treasures we have known. The glory and honor of the present world will not be lost but will be carried into the New Jerusalem (21:26). But the squalor and poverty, the immorality and impurity, which are so prevalent in the cities of this world, will be banished from the holy city. And so will the people who practice the unholy things that God hates (21:8, 27; 22:15).

This is the word of the Creator and Restorer, the Alpha and Omega, the A to Z, the Beginning and Conclusion of history. He is now busy making all things new (21:5). He begins with us, but he will not rest until he has renewed all things.

Four Horsemen of the Apocalypse, detail

—Edward Jakob Von Steinle, 1810-1886

CHAPTER 14

HOW TO EXPECT THE DAY OF HIS COMING

As we conclude our study, we should examine how we can maintain the right attitude while expecting the Lord. To rightly await his return, we must have a biblical understanding of our time in God's history of salvation.

In the Last Days

These are not "the last days" because the state of Israel has been established, as many preachers say. And these are not the last days because we now have the automobiles foretold in Nahum 2:4—"The chariots storm through the streets, rushing back and forth through the squares. They look like flaming torches; they dart about like lightning"—as is claimed in *Soon-Coming, World-Shaking Events!* (p. 14). These are not the end days because we have an explosion of information in fulfillment of Daniel 12:4—"Many will go here and there to increase knowledge." And not because we know about the Ebola virus, whose victims are described in Zechariah 14:12-15, or because we have the H-bomb described in 2 Peter 3:10, as John Hagee would like us to believe.

Instead, these are the last days "because [God] has spoken to us by his Son" (Heb. 1:2). The "fulfillment of the ages has come" on us (1 Cor. 10:11). And the Holy Spirit lives in each and every Christian (Acts 2:17). As revealed in the Bible, this is where we are in God's salvation history. And the only really new thing in store for us and the present world is the *parousia,* the coming of Christ.

Now God has entrusted to us the last Word for the last days. We must know and guard that gospel, not *as if* but *because* our lives depend on it.

Stay in Touch

The drone of ordinary life can make us forget the very purpose of living. Hundreds of thousands of people live their lives "eating, drinking, marrying and giving in marriage" (Matt. 24:38)—as did those who lived before the flood (v. 39). Notice that Jesus mentions no particular sins here. His point is that they lived under a warning and paid no attention. By the time they started to think about the purpose of life and the threat of disaster, it was too late.

Therefore "let us hold unswervingly to the hope we profess, for he who promised is faithful" (Heb. 10:23). We may not know *when* Jesus is coming but we know *that* he is coming. He is faithful and will do what he promised. "And let us consider how we may spur one another on toward love and good deeds"

(v. 24). We need to be part of a community of Christian people who are engaged in the work the Master gave us to do and who feel responsible for each other. "Let us not give up meeting together, as some are in the habit of doing, but let us encourage one another—and all the more as you see the Day approaching" (v. 25).

Be Mission Minded

These are the days of God's compassion in which he wants all people to come to the knowledge of the truth. We are the truth-tellers. The mission must shape the style of our churches and of our lives. But we should understand "mission" in the broad sense. The gospel must be proclaimed *extensively*—to our neighbors and to all parts of the globe, but also *intensively*; the Word of truth must be applied to every human activity and every part of our lives. The goal of the mission is "that God may be all in all" (1 Cor. 15:28) and "that in everything [Christ] might have the supremacy" (Col. 1:18). That's the "cultural mission"—an ongoing reordering of life. The mission places all things and all people in the service of the kingdom that is and that is coming.

In Light of Coming Events

We are called to holiness because our meeting with the Lord is in the near future. According to the Bible, his coming is never a reason for speculation or calculation. But it is always a reason for (moral) preparation. "The night is nearly over; the day is almost here. So let us put aside the deeds of darkness and put on the armor of light" (Rom. 13:12). Already we belong to the realm of light. The gospel awoke us from the stupor of sin and darkness: "since we belong to the day, let us be sober and put on the breastplate of faith and love and for a helmet the hope of salvation" (1 Thess. 5:8, NRSV).

The future rules our present behavior: "The end of all things is near. Therefore be clear minded and self-controlled so that you can pray" (1 Pet. 4:7). The clearheadedness that Scripture requires consists of awareness at all times that we are living between Christ's coming in grace and his appearance in glory. Those two poles mark the magnetic field in which we live (see Titus 2:11-13).

We know the terror of the day of judgment and the destruction a holy God will bring to the unprepared: "Since everything will be destroyed . . . what kind of people ought you to be? You ought to live holy and godly lives as you look forward to the day of God . . . " (2 Pet. 3:11-12). We must live holy lives because "when he appears, we shall be like him, for we shall see him as he is. Everyone who has this hope in him purifies himself, just as he is pure" (1 John 3:2-3).

We are invited to the wedding banquet. But we must dress up for the party, showing our appreciation for the coming meeting with our King (Matt. 22:1-14). Today's lifestyle is determined by tomorrow's feast.

Invest in Real Futures

Today you and I can make investments for the life to come. We can do so with money (Luke 16:9, 1 Tim. 6:18-19). It seems that the only money we can take along when we depart this present life is the part we give away. But our investment for the future concerns more than money. We must invest ourselves—our whole lives, full-time. That does not require spiritual sky-gazing. We should work with our hands so that we can be a help to others, said Paul to the Thessalonians.

Everyone will reap what she or he has sown. The present life is sowing time; the future age is harvesttime (Gal. 6:7-10). The path to a fruitful life is a life in Christ. By faith you and I are in Christ and whatever we do is done "in the Lord." We "marry in the Lord," we do our labor "in the Lord," and finally "we fall asleep in Jesus." Such a life lasts forever.

Many things that ask for our attention in this life are not worth it. But if we are busy with that which is true, noble, right, lovely, admirable, excellent, and praiseworthy (Phil. 4:8), then we are involved in things that will last forever.

And whatever we do out of love for Jesus will be remembered by our eternal God.

Pray, Praise, and Carry On

Prayer must be learned. Not every cry to the sky is a prayer. Jewish rabbis and Christian teachers used to teach their disciples how to pray (Luke 11:1). Our Teacher taught us how to speak to Abba: "Father, hallowed be your name, your kingdom come" (Luke 11:2). Christ wants this prayer to be a model for our prayer life. It's a kingdom prayer. We ask that our Father's name be respected and adored by us and by everybody. That will become a reality when the Father's kingdom has come. And the kingdom has come when his will is done on earth as God is already obeyed in heaven. We pray with a kingdom perspective. While we seek the kingdom first, we also trust that our Abba will give us our daily bread, forgive our daily debts, and uphold us in the daily spiritual struggle.

Many people, especially young people, must still learn that praying for the coming of the kingdom (and of the King) does not mean that we are asking for the end of the party. We're praying for the feast to start! Therefore we must often speak to each other about the hope that we have.

Add praise to your prayers. Most of the time we are beggars before God: "Give me, help me, bless me, please, please . . . " When we praise, we no longer ask, but we have something to give. Already here on the battlefield, we begin to sing the doxology. In her song of praise, the church of God has a foretaste of the end.

It's the grace of God, received by prayer and extolled in praise, that gives meaning to our ordinary lives. We have extraordinary promises but we spend our lives doing ordinary things. And that's all right. Jesus spent most of his years in the flesh doing carpenter's work.

Suddenly we will see him. We will laugh and shout for joy. All of us caterpillars will turn into butterflies. Every Cinderella will become a princess. The whole world will see what God's grace can do with ordinary people.

BIBLIOGRAPHY

GENERAL

Note: Most of what I know about New Testament theology I learned from Herman Ridderbos. Since I use his writings in their original (Dutch) language, I do not always acknowledge his books as my sources. The two books by Ridderbos listed below are the main sources I used that are available in English translation.

Bavinck, Herman. *The Last Things*. Grand Rapids, Mich.: Baker Books, 1996.

> This book and those by Berkouwer and Ridderbos listed in this section are works by Dutch authors in the Reformed tradition that are available in English.

Berkouwer, G. C. *The Return of Christ*. Grand Rapids, Mich.: Eerdmans, 1972.

Cullman, Oscar. *Christ and Time*. London: SCM Press, 1965.

Hoekema, Anthony A. *The Bible and the Future*. Grand Rapids, Mich.: Eerdmans, 1979.

> A more comprehensive but still popular treatment of the topics addressed in this book.

Kümmel, W. G. *Promise and Fulfillment*. London: SCM Press, 1956.

Ridderbos, Herman N. *Paul: An Outline of His Theology*. Grand Rapids, Mich.: Eerdmans, 1975.

_____. *The Coming of the Kingdom*. Philadelphia: Presbyterian and Reformed Publishing Company, 1975.

ON MILLENNIALISM

Clouse, Robert G. (editor). *The Meaning of the Millennium*. Downers Grove: InterVarsity Press, 1977.

> The literature on millennialism is overwhelming. This book presents a popular overview of the four kinds.

Grenz, Stanley J. *The Millennial Maze*. Downers Grove: InterVarsity Press, 1992.

> Gives a more up-to-date overview.

ON AMILLENNIALISM

Adams, Jay E. *The Time Is at Hand*. Philadelphia: Presbyterian and Reformed Publishing Company, 1973.

Allis, Oswald T. *Prophecy and the Church*. Philadelphia: Presbyterian and Reformed Publishing Company, 1974.

Hoekema, Anthony A. *The Bible and the Future*. Grand Rapids, Mich.: Eerdmans, 1979.

> Cited above, the best source on so-called amillennialism that I've found.

Travis, Steven. *I Believe in the Second Coming of Jesus*. Grand Rapids, Mich.: Eerdmans, 1982.

ON POSTMILLENNIALISM

DeMar, Gary. *Last Days Madness: The Folly of Trying to Predict when Christ Will Return*. Brentwood, Tenn.: Wolgemuth and Hyatt, 1991.

> The best-known writer for this branch of millennialism is Lorraine Boettner, but DeMar's book is an easy read.

ON DISPENSATIONAL PREMILLENNIALISM

Lindsey, Hal. *The Late Great Planet Earth*. Grand Rapids, Mich.: Zondervan, 1970.

> A popularized version of dispensationalism and the rapture.

Poythress, Vern S. *Understanding Dispensationalists*. Phillipsburg, N.J.: Presbyterian and Reformed Publishing Company, 1994.

> A critical, irenic, and scholarly look at dispensationalism.

Ryrie, Charles C. *Dispensationalism Today*. Chicago: Moody Press, 1965.

Walvoord, John F. *The Millennial Kingdom*. Grand Rapids, Mich.: Dunham, 1959.

_____. *The Rapture Question*. Grand Rapids, Mich.: Zondervan, 1979.

ON NONDISPENSATIONAL PREMILLENNIALISM

Ladd, George Eldon. *The Last Things*. Grand Rapids, Mich.: Eerdmans, 1978.

> For a succinct statement of Ladd's position, see his contribution in *The Meaning of the Millennium*, mentioned above.

ON PROGRESSIVE DISPENSATIONALISM

Saucy, Robert L. *The Case for Progressive Dispensationalism*. Grand Rapids, Mich.: Zondervan, 1993.

> A good source for those interested in a theological treatment.

ON FUNDAMENTALISM AND DISPENSATIONALISM IN THE CULTURAL HISTORY OF NORTH AMERICA

Boyer, Paul. *When Time Shall Be No More: Prophecy Belief in Modern American Culture*. Cambridge/London: Harvard University Press, 1992.

Marsden, George, M. *Fundamentalism and American Culture: The Shaping of Twentieth Century Evangelicalism 1870-1925*. New York/Oxford: Oxford University Press, 1980.

ON THE RELATIONSHIP BETWEEN ISRAEL AND THE CHURCH

Hendriksen, William. *Israel in Prophecy*. Grand Rapids, Mich.: Baker, 1968.

Gives a popular reply to Walvoord's thesis given in the source listed below.

Holwerda, David E. *Jesus and Israel: One Covenant or Two?* Grand Rapids, Mich.: Eerdmans, 1995.

A definitive treatment of the subject.

Walvoord, John F. *Israel in Prophecy*. Grand Rapids, Mich.: Zondervan, 1962.

See also the books listed above on dispensational millennialism by this and other authors.

ON THE INTERPRETATION OF THE OLD TESTAMENT IN THE NEW TESTAMENT ERA

Green, Joel B. *How to Read Prophecy*. Downers Grove: InterVarsity Press, 1984.

More accessible than the scholarly, foundational treatment given this subject by E. Ellis.

Hughes, Philip E. *Interpreting Prophecy*. Grand Rapids, Mich.: Eerdmans, 1976.

BOOKS MENTIONED IN THIS STUDY

Adams, Jay E. *The Time Is at Hand.* Phillipsburg: P&R Publishing, 1973.

Bavinck, Herman. *The Last Things.* Grand Rapids, Mich.: Baker, 1996.

Berkhof, Hendrikus. *Christ, the Meaning of History.* (Tr. by L. Buurman.) Richmond: John Knox, 1966.

Berkouwer, G. C. *The Return of Christ.* Grand Rapids, Mich.: Eerdmans, 1972.

Blaising, Craig A. and Darrel L. Block. *Progressive Dispensationalism.* Victor/Bridgepoint, 1993.

Boer, Harry R. *The Book of Revelation.* Grand Rapids, Mich.: Eerdmans, 1979.

Boyer, Paul. *When Time Shall Be No More.* Cambridge: Harvard University Press, 1992.

Bruce, F. F. *The Hard Sayings of Jesus.* Downers Grove: InterVarsity Press, 1983.

_____. *The Letter of Paul to the Romans.* Tyndale New Testament Commentaries. Leicester and Grand Rapids, Mich.: InterVarsity Press and Eerdmans, 1987.

Bultema, Harry. *Maranatha!* (English translation by Cornelius Lambregtse.) Grand Rapids, Mich.: Kregel, 1985.

Calvin, John. *Institutes of the Christian Religion.* (John T. McNeill ed., tr. by Ford Lewis Battles.) Philadelphia: The Westminster Press, 1960.

Camping, Harold. *1994?* New York: Vantage Press, 1992.

Chafer, Lewis S. *Systematic Theology, Vol. 2 (abridged ed.).* Victor Books, Scripture Press, 1988.

Cooper, John W. *Body, Soul and Life Everlasting: Biblical Anthropology and the Monism-Dualism Debate.* Grand Rapids, Mich.: Eerdmans, 1989.

Cullman, Oscar. *Christ and Time.* (Tr. by Floyd V. Filson.) London: SCM Press, 1962.

DeMar, Gary. *Last Days Madness: The Folly of Trying to Predict when Christ Will Return.* Brentwood, Tenn.: Wohlgemut & Hyatt, 1991.

De Ridder, Richard R. *God Has Not Rejected His People.* Grand Rapids, Mich.: Baker, 1977.

Ellison, H. L. *The Mystery of Israel.* Grand Rapids, Mich.: Eerdmans, 1966.

Green, Joel B. *How to Read Prophecy.* Downers Grove: InterVarsity Press, 1984.

Grenz, Stanley, J. *The Millennial Maze.* Downers Grove: InterVarsity Press, 1992.

Gundry, Robert H. *The Church and the Tribulation.* Grand Rapids, Mich.: Zondervan, 1973.

Hagee, John. *Beginning of the End.* Nashville: Thomas Nelson, 1996.

Hendriksen, William. *Israel in Prophecy.* Grand Rapids, Mich.: Baker, 1974.

_____. *New Testament Commentary, I and II Thessalonians.* Grand Rapids, Mich.: Baker, 1955.

Hoekema, Anthony A. *The Bible and the Future*. Grand Rapids, Mich.: Eerdmans, 1979.

Holwerda, David E. *Jesus and Israel, One Covenant or Two?* Grand Rapids, Mich.: Eerdmans, 1995.

Kistemaker, Simon J. *New Testament Commentary: Peter and Jude*. Grand Rapids, Mich.: Baker, 1987.

Kromminga, D. H. *The Millennium in the Church*. Grand Rapids, Mich.: Eerdmans, 1945.

Kuyvenhoven, Andrew. *Comfort and Joy: A Study of the Heidelberg Catechism*. Grand Rapids, Mich.: CRC Publications, 1988.

Ladd, George E. *The Last Things*. Grand Rapids, Mich.: Eerdmans, 1978.

Lightfoot, J. B. and J. R. Harmer. *The Apostolic Fathers*. Grand Rapids, Mich.: Baker, 1984.

Lindsey, Hal. *The Late Great Planet Earth*. Grand Rapids, Mich.: Zondervan, 1970.

MacPherson, David. *The Unbelievable Pre-Trib Origin*. Kansas City: Heart of America Bible Society, 1973.

Maier, Paul L. *Josephus, the Essential Writings*. Grand Rapids, Mich.: Kregel, 1988.

Marsden, George, M. *Fundamentalism and American Culture*. New York/Oxford: Oxford University Press, 1980.

Marshall, Paul. *Their Blood Cries Out: The Worldwide Tragedy of Modern Christians Who Are Dying for Their Faith*. Dallas: Word Publishing, 1997.

Moltmann, Jürgen, *The Way of Jesus Christ*. Minneapolis: Fortress Press, 1993.

Moore, Marvin. *The Antichrist and the New World Order*. Boise: Pacific Press, 1960.

Morris, Leon. *The Epistles of Paul to the Thessalonians*. Tyndale New Testament Commentaries. Grand Rapids, Mich.: Eerdmans, 1960.

Moulton, James H. and George Milligan. *The Vocabulary of the Greek New Testament*. Grand Rapids, Mich.: Eerdmans, 1960.

Murray, Iain. *The Puritan Hope*. London: Banner of Trust, 1971.

New Scofield Study Bible, 1967 and the *New Scofield Reference Bible,* 1989.

Olson, V. Norskov, ed. *The Advent Hope in Scripture and History*. Washington: Review and Herald Publishing Association, 1987.

Payne, J. Barton. *The Prophecy Map of World History*. New York: Harper & Row, 1974.

Pentecost, J. Dwight. *Thy Kingdom Come*. Victor Books, Scripture Press, 1990.

Peters, George N. H. *The Theocratic Kingdom*. Grand Rapids, Mich.: Kregel, 1952.

Pieters, Albertus. *The Seed of Abraham*. Grand Rapids, Mich.: Eerdmans, 1950.

Potok, Chaim. *My Name Is Asher Lev*. New York: Fawcett Crest, 1991.

Poythress, Vern S. *Understanding Dispensationalists*. Phillipsburg: P&R Publishing, 1994.

Rottenberg, Isaac C. "Should There Be a Christian Witness to the Jews?" *Christian Century,* April 13, 1977.

Ryrie, Charles C. *The Final Countdown.* Wheaton: Scripture Press, 1982.

Schulte Nordholt, Jan Willem. *So Much Sky.* (tr. by Henrietta Ten Harmsel.) Grand Rapids, Mich.: Eerdmans, 1994.

Soon-Coming, World-Shaking Events! Phoenix: Christian Missionary Society, 1978.

Travis, Stephen H. *Christian Hope and the Future.* Downers Grove: InterVarsity Press, 1983.

_____. *I Believe in the Second Coming of Jesus.* Grand Rapids, Mich.: Eerdmans, 1982.

Vos, Geerhardus. *The Pauline Eschatology.* Phillipsburg: P&R Publishing, 1991.

Walker, Williston, *A History of the Christian Church.* New York: Charles Scribner's Sons, 1970.

Walvoort, John F. *Israel in Prophecy.* Grand Rapids, Mich.: Zondervan, 1962.

_____. *The Rapture Question.* Grand Rapids, Mich.: Zondervan, 1979.

Whisenant, Edgar. *88 Reasons Why the Rapture Will Be in 1988.* Nashville: World Bible Society, 1988.

_____. *The Final Shout.* Nashville: World Bible Society, 1989.